1. An Undivided Heart

AN UNDIVIDED HEART
Making Sense of Celibate Chastity

AN UNDIVIDED HEART

Making Sense of Celibate Chastity

SEAN D. SAMMON, FMS

ALBA · HOUSE NEW · YORK

SOCIETY OF ST. PAUL, 2187 VICTORY BLVD., STATEN ISLAND, NEW YORK 10314

Library of Congress Cataloging-in-Publication Data

Sammon, Sean D., 1947-
An undivided heart : making sense of celibate chastity / Sean D. Sammon.
p. cm.
Includes bibliographical references.
ISBN 0-8189-0674-X
1. Celibacy — Catholic Church. 2. Chastity. 3. Catholic Church — Clergy. 4. Monastic and religious life. I. Title.
BV4390.S25 1993
253'.2 — dc20 93-3852
CIP

Produced and designed in the United States of America by the Fathers and Brothers of the Society of St. Paul, 2187 Victory Boulevard, Staten Island, New York 10314, as part of their communications apostolate.

ISBN: 0-8189-0674-X

Printing Information:

Current Printing - first digit 1 2 3 4 5 6 7 8 9 10

Year of Current Printing - first year shown

1993 1994 1995 1996 1997 1998

DEDICATION

John Edward Kerrigan, Jr.
with gratitude for his friendship

CONTENTS

INTRODUCTION

What is the purpose of this book? Something quite simple: to help men and women called to a life of celibate chastity better understand this way of being a sexual person. These are not easy times for those who choose to live out their sexuality in this manner. Misunderstandings about the subject, distorted notions about human sexuality in general, and the recent and loudly touted so-called "Sexual Revolution" have done little to encourage celibate chaste people or offer others an incentive to join them. The ideas presented in this book will, I hope, add something useful to today's ongoing conversation about the topic.

The text includes four chapters plus this introduction and an epilogue. An appendix on the topic of child sexual abuse is also included. The first chapter, entitled *First Things First*, offers some introductory notions about human sexuality and celibate chastity; it also provides a context for our discussion by examining both topics within the structure of the life cycle. In short order, it becomes clear that a person cannot live a life of celibate chastity at age fifty five in the same way he or she did at age twenty eight; so also people's understanding and experience of human sexuality change as they grow older.

Chapter II, *Two Sides of the Same Coin: Identity and Intimacy*, takes a look at the concept of personal identity and cites its importance in any relationship of intimacy. This chapter also identifies some factors that enhance and others that pose a barrier to mature intimacy; in addition, relationships between men and women and the masculine/feminine sides of each of us receive some treatment.

Sex and Sanity, the book's third chapter, presents a few ideas about healthy psychosexual growth. It also answers the question: just what factors interfere with this type of development? Additional topics treated in Chapter III include sexual identity and sexual orientation.

Finally, the fourth chapter, *An Undivided Search for God*, examines the topic of celibate chastity. Terms are defined; various understandings of celibate chastity--the law, a discipline, a functional value, and a gift or gospel value--are treated. The central point of this chapter is quite simple: a person's celibate chastity must be rooted deeply in the spiritual life. Marianist David Fleming puts it this way: religious experience is the key to the meaningful living out of celibate chastity. This section closes with a discussion about two areas: stages of growth in a life of celibate chastity; characteristics common among those who are at home with this way of being a sexual person.

I write about the topic of celibate chastity from the perspective of psychology. With only a layperson's knowledge of medicine, moral theology, and philosophy, I leave it to others to give life and voice to what these disciplines will contribute to our conversation about the subject. I do believe, however, that ethical and moral values must be at the heart of any person's sexual life; without them, it becomes something less than human.

This book has an audience beyond priests and men and women religious. Many Catholic and Protestant laypeople, living the single life or single again, also believe they are called to a life of celibate chastity; the ideas presented herein will, I hope, enrich their own reflection on this dimension of their life.

The question of optional celibacy for Roman Catholic priests is not addressed in these pages. As a Church we are long overdue for a full discussion of that topic; this book, however, is not the place for that conversation. Instead, it's written for those of us who believe we are called to live out our sexuality in a celibate chaste way.

Reflection questions are interspersed throughout each chapter; they should help you personalize the material presented and apply it to your own life. It's usually helpful to jot down some of your reactions and responses to each question; in this way, you'll have them for later reference. A list of additional readings appears at the end of each chapter; it will help you supplement the material found in the text.

No book comes to life without the assistance of others; this one is no exception to that rule. I'm grateful to those who read chapters while they were in the making and offered many helpful revisions. In particular, I want to thank Jane Amirault, RGS, Craig F. Evans, ACSW, Nuala Harty, OLA, Paul Hennessy, CFC, Kenneth Hogan, FMS, Kathleen E. Kelley, PhD, John E. Kerrigan, Jr., John Malich, FMS, John Nash, FMS, Rea McDonnell, SSND, John Perring-Mulligan, Hank Sammon, FMS, and Mary Sammon.

A word of thanks also to Marie Kraus, SND; she not only read the text but edited the book throughout. If it's easy to read, clear, and helpful, you need to thank those listed above.

Brother Aloysius Milella, SSP, my editor at Alba House, deserves special mention. He and I discussed the idea of this book several years ago. About eighteen months back, he wrote to tell me that he had "lit a candle in the window" waiting for the manuscript. As you can see, he is a very patient man, and one who quietly prodded me along; my thanks to him.

This work is dedicated to John E. Kerrigan, Jr. He encouraged, cajoled, and finally persuaded me to put the book together. On many a camping trip, in the U.S. and Canadian Rockies, we've discussed a number of the ideas found in the following pages. John has been a dear friend for almost a quarter century. He is also very much a brother to me; I'm grateful on both accounts.

Sean D. Sammon, FMS
January 25, 1993
Watertown, MA

CHAPTER I

FIRST THINGS FIRST

First, a story!

It's about a young woman who wrote home from college to her middle-aged parents. They hadn't heard from her in quite a while; snatching the envelope from the mailbox, they tore it open and began to read their daughter's letter:

> Dear Mom and Dad,
>
> Sorry I haven't written in such a long time but there have been some problems here at school. To begin with, the dormitory burned down! I felt a bit responsible for this fire: my roommate was smoking marijuana at the time and in her confusion may have started the blaze.
>
> Don't worry about me, though, I do have a place to live; my boyfriend invited me to move in with him. He's a nice guy who dropped out of school recently. At the moment, he's busy picking up odd jobs here and there with the hope of getting enough experience to work at his father's gas station in Alaska. I will be joining him there at the end of the semester. Don't be too concerned about either of us; he has promised to marry me before the baby arrives!

The middle-aged couple stopped here! The content of their daughter's letter was not what they had expected; before continuing to read, both sat down. The letter went on:

> Mom and Dad, the dorm did not burn down; neither my roommate nor I am involved with marijuana or drugs of any kind. I do have a boy friend; he's a rather nice guy and still in school. While it's a good relationship, we've made no plans about the future. He has no intention of moving to Alaska; neither do I. Also, I am not pregnant. However, I did get a "D" in chemistry and just wanted to put that fact into its proper context!

Contexts are important; they help us frame a question or topic and give us perspective on an issue. Without doubt, the one provided by the young woman just mentioned certainly helped her parents appreciate the significance of the "D" she got in chemistry!

This chapter, foundational to the book, sets the stage for our discussion about human sexuality and celibate chastity; both topics will be introduced and then explored within the context of human growth and development over the course of life. As we age, most of us grow into a greater understanding and deeper appreciation of our human sexuality and our celibate chastity. At age forty-five, for example, we are different people sexually than we were at twenty-five; just as those of us who are sisters, priests, and brothers grow over time in our appreciation and understanding of the vows of poverty and obedience, so also do we grow into the experience of celibate chastity. On the day we make this vow, we most often have little more than an intellectual understanding of just what it will entail; we simply cannot live out our life of celibate chastity at fifty-two in the same way we did at twenty-two.

THE IMPORTANCE OF HAVING A CONTEXT FOR OUR DISCUSSION OF SEXUALITY AND CELIBATE CHASTITY

A. Human Sexuality

Any discussion about human sexuality first needs a context, a frame of reference that will help give us perspective on the topic. For example, today many people have a constricted view of human sexuality; they equate it with genital sexual behavior. The word intimacy is often used in the same way: if a person says that he or she has an intimate relationship with someone, many of us might presume they are sleeping together! These narrow frames of reference fail to help us appreciate the complexity and richness of our human sexuality.

James B. Nelson, Professor of Christian Ethics at United Theological Seminary of the Twin Cities, takes a different approach; he makes a distinction between sex and sexuality. The first term applies to a biologically-based need oriented toward procreation, pleasure, and release of tension; it aims at genital activity culminating in orgasm and focuses upon erotic phenomena of a largely genital nature.

Sexuality, in contrast, could include all that was just said about sex, but it also embraces a great deal more. It includes our way of being in the world as a male or female and the attitudes and characteristics, culturally defined as masculine and feminine, that we appropriate over time. The word sexuality also involves our affectional orientation toward people of the opposite and same sex and our attitudes toward our body and those of others.

Ultimately, though, Nelson points out that the notion of sexuality captures our basic human need to reach out, both physically and spiritually, to embrace others; it expresses God's intention that we find out in relationship what it means to be human and spiritual. Yes, sexuality is intrinsic to our relationship with other people and with God; it has much more to do with self-transcendence than with self-fulfillment. A far cry, isn't it, from equating human sexuality with genital sexual behavior.

B. Celibate Chastity

Discussion about the meaning of celibate chastity also suffers without a context. For example, when asked why they chose to live a life of celibate chastity, many men and women religious will answer: "For the sake of the kingdom; in order to love everyone and not just one person; to be more available." Then they take a deep breath and hope that no one else asks any more questions! In contrast, understanding that a life of celibate chastity is one way of being a sexual person provides a much wider context in which to explore the topic.

While the topic of celibate chastity will be discussed more fully in Chapter IV, it's important to realize that not only priests, sisters, and brothers live out their sexuality in this way; many single and single again people do also. For example, some men and women who spend their lives caring for an aged parent or relative believe that they also have the gift of celibate chastity.

THE LIFE CYCLE AS A CONTEXT FOR OUR DISCUSSION ABOUT SEXUALITY AND CELIBATE CHASTITY

Have you ever found yourself asking any of the following questions: What am I doing with my life? Is it possible for me to live in a way that best combines my talents, current desires, values, and aspirations? What do I truly get from and give to others? Does anyone really care about me; do I really care about anyone else? Another blunt question quickly summarizes those listed above: If I were to die today, what in my life would be left unlived?

We often ask questions like these when in the midst of life change. During any transition we run through this rather sobering inventory: Where am I going? Who am I aside from what I do? Do I love anyone? Does anyone love me? All these questions address issues of personal identity and intimacy.

A middle-aged woman religious, for example, about to celebrate her silver jubilee wondered whom she would invite. An author and teacher, she was successful in her work and respected by her colleagues. However, working on the invitation list, this woman realizes that she has no close friends, no relationships of intimacy, only colleagues and acquaintances. Uncovering this fact, she also finds herself re-evaluating her priorities, work, and life commitment. The process is a painful one; she feels fragmented and finds that in addition to her lack of personal friends, she has also neglected her interior life. As this woman turns her sights away from the external and toward her inner world, she does not need to discover something new in her life but rather grow to see her life in a new way. She needs to attend to her interior life, discover herself anew, allow for the possibility of some intimacy.

What lies at the heart of all our concerns about identity and intimacy is a spiritual question: On whom or what do I set my heart? The gospels express it just a bit differently: Where does your treasure lie? While this spiritual question comes to the fore during each period of life change and transition, my age and time in life influence the shape it will take.

THE LIFE CYCLE

Let's arbitrarily divide the seasons of life into five eras of twenty to twenty-five years each: pre-adulthood, and early, middle, late, and late late adulthood.

A. Pre-adulthood

The first era, pre-adulthood, includes infancy, childhood, and adolescence. What is the message of this time in life? Growth, change, and development are expected and encouraged. Consider, for example, our concern about an infant who fails to walk or talk by a prescribed age; we worry about the child's failure to reach these developmental milestones or fret about possible retardation. Adolescence is another time of tremendous personal change; teenage love relationships, after all, tend to be short-term and tumultuous.

Even though we easily accept infancy, childhood, and adolescence as times of great and visible change, conventional wisdom suggests that around age eighteen or nineteen, a curtain falls and we have a fully fashioned adult; having "grown up," a person should be well able to handle whatever the future holds.

To understand human development in this way is a bit like viewing men and women as automobiles: put together in the factory of infancy, childhood, and adolescence, they are road tested about age eighteen or nineteen; any change after that time is to be considered a malfunction!

Significant growth, change, and development take place after pre-adulthood. For one thing, an ability to reflect on our life experience begins to flourish once we exit the teenage years; the developmental work of adulthood, then, is at least as important as the groundwork laid between infancy and late adolescence.

B. Early Adulthood

Early adulthood, getting underway during the late teens and continuing until the mid forties, includes some of the most stressful years of life. For those of us younger than forty-five, it might provide small consolation to claim citizenship in early adulthood.

a. Novice Adulthood

The years from the late teens until the mid-thirties make up a sub-stage of early adulthood often referred to as novice adulthood. What is the challenge of this time in life? To address four tasks of maturity, by developing a life dream, mentoring relationships, an apostolate or life work, and relationships of intimacy. There is good and bad news about this challenge. The bad news: four developmental tasks face us; the good news: we can be expected to address only one or two during these years.

Novice adulthood is that time in life when we learn what it means to be an adult. Many young men and women, however, feel as though they are impersonating an adult; while functioning as grown-ups, they believe that it is just a matter of time before they are found out to be impostors. For example, a young diocesan priest, ordained at age twenty-six, related the following story. A few weeks after ordination, he found himself sitting in the rectory office one evening; a middle-aged married couple came in for some counseling about their relationship. The young priest tried to listen, but found himself distracted by this recurring thought: these people are old enough to be my parents; it will not be very long before they discover that I simply do not know what I am doing!

1. Some of Novice Adulthood's Developmental Tasks

Let's look briefly at a few of the developmental tasks that mark novice adulthood. To begin with, forming and living out one's life dream is an important challenge of this period. Often vague at first, the dream answers this question: What am I going to do with my life? For those who give it a place in their life, this dream becomes an important motivating influence; those who betray it face later consequences.

A young man, for example, struggles with two possible life directions: one that expresses his dream, another that fails to do so. He can move in the first direction or allow himself to be pushed away from his dream by parents, or external factors such as money or a personality trait or a special talent. In betraying his dream, this young man may succeed in life; having lost touch with it, however, his motivation and sense of purpose will die eventually. At midlife he will have to revisit his early dream and try, once again, to bring his life into line with its spirit.

Evelyn and James Whitehead, a developmental psychologist and theologian respectively, point to another aspect of our life dream: our vocation or, put another way, God's dream for us. During novice adulthood, we are all called upon to imagine, both psychologically and spiritually, what our life is to be about; discovering what God has in mind for us is an important part of that process.

Vocations, however, are not "once and for all" calls; no, they are lifelong conversations. Fidelity has to entail more than recalling an early invitation; at midlife, for example, I must still be able to believe that God is up to something in my life.

Mentoring relationships are another important part of novice adulthood. Serving as both parents and peers, mentors provide young adults with counsel and support; they are often models by their own achievements and way of life.

Who are important mentors? Some spiritual directors, teachers, colleagues and friends, religious superiors and those men and women who initiate us into religious life and priesthood by their example. Where do they find their satisfaction? In furthering the development of others and facilitating their efforts to form and live out their life's dreams.

2. *Intimacy, Human Sexuality, and Celibate Chastity during Novice Adulthood*

During novice adulthood we are young in our understanding and experience of intimacy, human sexuality, and celibate chastity. A number of researchers, for example, suggest that while some young men and women experience deep loving relationships during this stage of development, for many, mature intimacy is just not possible until later in life. Uncertainty and confusion often surround young adult sexuality, and the rich spirituality that lies at the heart of genuine celibate chaste living is often not available until midlife.

As some priests and men and women religious approach the end of their twenties, however, questions about intimacy take on greater import. A number fall in love for the first time. This experience, often one of infatuation, is an important step toward building loving adult relationships with other men and women.

For those who experience a deep loving relationship during novice adulthood, many feelings are involved: joy, jealousy, preoccupation, disappointment, a rare tenderness. The relationship transforms many of those involved; their commitments grow stronger. Their communities benefit also: in living with celibate chaste men and women who can express affection spontaneously and be unguarded in their relationships, other people grow to be more themselves.

Healthy priesthood and religious life include caring relationships that grow over time. Working together on projects and in ministry, for example, many young religious and priests find that care for another person is awakened. With time, it grows and deepens. Such love relationships can, at times, frighten others within the community or diocese; they move to limit them and express concern and disapproval. These reactions are not very helpful. Few people want to live without love;

those striving to live a celibate chaste life also need to be able to love others in a passionate and human way.

In the face of a deep loving relationship, however, other young religious and priests begin to question their earlier commitments. One thirty-year-old religious brother framed his dilemma this way: "Because of a deep loving relationship in my life I have come to realize my need for intimacy; right now, I am struggling to find out whether I can live a celibate chaste life without the type of intense intimacy found only in marriage."

A sexual awakening can accompany the experience of deep love for some sisters, priests, and brothers: they become aware, often for the first time, of the full force and power of their sexuality. As a consequence, past understandings about celibate chastity are called into question. Some start to realize they can be effective apostles without living a life of celibate chastity; others come to understand that a loving relationship with another person is one way to a loving relationship with God. More will be said about sexual awakenings in Chapter III.

When the loving relationship is between two men or two women, fear and suspicion can arise. Our society is burdened with homophobia; misunderstandings about homosexuality also exist. Early on in life, these factors can cause gay men and lesbian women to be uncomfortable with their sexual feelings. As a consequence, a number of them do not grow to be at home with their sexual orientation until late in novice adulthood. This topic will also be explored more fully in Chapter III.

Mourning the loss of a biological family of one's own making is another challenge that many priests, men and women religious, and others who choose a life of celibate chastity face during novice adulthood. Parenting children is the work of early adulthood; around age thirty, priests, sisters, brothers and other celibate chaste people become aware of this fact: some contemporaries are forming families and mothering and fathering children. As a result, some of the consequences of an earlier choice for celibate chastity begin to unfold. In embracing the loss of parenthood, they are better able to redirect their creative energies into other areas of their life; if they refuse to grieve, that energy will remain forever trapped within them.

Whatever decisions they make about relationships and the developmental tasks of the period, novice adults need the support of mentors as they search for the place of intimacy in their lives. Though middle adulthood may present the best opportunity for free and loving relationships to mature, many of them have their roots in the years before.

Echoing theologian Norman Pittenger, I'd suggest that human sexuality provides the foundation for our capacity to enter into life-enhancing and life-enriching relationships, full of the possibility for people to become what God would have them become: fulfilled, integrated, sharing, and free recipients of divine love. Human sexuality has to be the central clue to what God is up to in my life and in our world.

REFLECTION QUESTIONS

Pause here for a few moments and reflect back on what you've just read; then spend some time answering the following questions. This exercise will help you integrate the above material into your day-to-day life.

As you work, you may want to jot down a few notes about your thoughts or journal in response to each question. Consider sharing your findings with a friend, a trusted colleague, some members of your community, a counselor or spiritual director.

1. People grow and change over the course of life. In what ways are you different today from who you were ten years ago? What led to the changes? What are the rewards and disappointments of this time in your life?

2. These questions occur throughout the course of life.
   a. What am I doing with my life?
   b. Is it possible for me to live in a way that best combines my talents, current desires, values, and aspirations?
   c. What do I truly get from and give to others?
   d. Does anyone really care about me; do I really care about anyone else?
   e. If I were to die today, what in my life would be left unlived?

   Spend some time considering each question. How would you answer it today? How might you have answered it ten or fifteen years ago?
3. Spend some time trying to identify your life dream. What are its elements? How have you been able to give it a place in your life? Who were the mentors that helped with this task — name them and describe the ways in which they assisted.
4. What has been (was) your experience of intimacy during early adulthood? Spend some time considering the joys and disappointments associated with these experiences — what have they taught you?

Now let's continue with Chapter I as we consider middle adulthood.

C. Middle Adulthood

By midlife, most of us can appreciate the wisdom of Oscar Wilde's observation: "The gods have two ways of dealing harshly with us: the first is to deny us our dreams, and the second is to grant them." Midlife is a time for taking stock, for removing rose-colored glasses and calling things by their right names. Dante said it well in *The Divine Comedy*: "In the middle of the journey of my life, I came to myself within a dark wood where the straight way was lost. Ah, how hard it is to tell of that wood, savage and harsh and dense. The thought of it renews my fears. So bitter is it that death is hardly more."

The challenges of midlife, those years between the early forties and mid-sixties, are many: facing personal mortality; bridging the gap between early and middle adulthood; trying to pull together all those disparate parts that make up each of us. Midlife also brings new roles and responsibilities and is a time for life re-evaluation. Saul Bellow's fictional character, Moses Herzog, puts it this way: "Maybe I am going through a change in outlook." In crossing the line between early and middle adulthood, this midlife man lost his easy sense of immortality; he knew more clearly than ever before that he had probably lived more years already than the number that lay ahead for him. This knowledge made a difference: Moses Herzog realized that he couldn't live someone else's life; the values and standards that would guide him henceforth had to be his own.

A middle-aged woman religious, for example, develops a relationship with a man. With time they grow closer; the bond between them deepens. This woman imagines what it would be like to spend her life with this man. The relationship introduces her to aspects of herself of which she was not aware. Former obligations and present commitments come under close scrutiny. She has many feelings: wonder, deep affection, confusion, loss, fear, guilt, fulfillment.

This woman also experiences a loss of her old identity; former ways of self-understanding no longer make any sense. For a period of time, her life is in turmoil as she attempts to meet community obligations and maintain this important relationship. Eventually, she comes to understand herself in a new way. The process of change has been painful, its fruits worthwhile: a transformed outlook on life, acknowledged needs, confirmed awareness of God's presence and action in her life.

At midlife we need to shed the illusions we have about ourselves, others, and the way the world should work, and put our efforts into working on the developmental tasks of the period. About this time we also come to realize that without roots in the spiritual life, celibate chastity has no meaning; the spiritual life is at the core of genuine celibate chaste living.

Consider a religious brother who spent most of his early apostolic life involved in a number of distracting activities. Burning the candle at both ends, he forced certain aspects of his life — friends, leisure time, spirituality — into second place. While quite effective in ministry, his celibate chastity has become little more than functional. Although successful, around midlife this man begins to wonder what he is doing with his life. The meaning of his celibate chastity, the significance of his life, his very self — all are strangers to him. Solitude, if embraced, will introduce him to these fellow travelers.

Finally, about midlife some men and women grow to realize that they are survivors of incest and other forms of child abuse. Trauma that gets buried in the psyche can re-emerge decades after the fact. What triggers this awareness? A news report or TV program about the subject; the discovery that another member of one's family is also a survivor. One middle-aged woman reported ignorance about her abuse until the day she had her first body massage. Suddenly, as the masseuse touched her thigh, the memories erupted within her. More will be said about the topic of child sexual abuse in the Appendix of this book.

An understanding of a few of midlife's developmental tasks is also important for our discussion of human sexuality and celibate chastity. What are they? The need to develop a greater care for others, a deeper sense of interiority, and an integration of our masculine and feminine sides. Let's say a word about each.

a. Care for Others

Caught between two generations, most midlifers find themselves responsible for both older and younger people. Middle-aged men and women, however, usually have little opportunity to choose those for whom they will be responsible or how this task is to be carried out!

Mentoring, that experience of being neither a parent nor peer but both at the same time, offers many midlifers a unique opportunity to expand their care for others. Exercising this role with a younger generation is fairly straightforward and it helps to facilitate the answer to this question, "What am I going to do with my adult life?" Mentors provide encouragement for young people and, at times, a life worthy of emulation.

The task of mentoring an older generation is not defined so clearly. Some guidelines, however, do exist. To begin with, mentors can help older people rediscover parts of themselves lost when they made earlier life decisions. In making those choices, many, by necessity, had to neglect aspects of their personality. During life's second half, they can rediscover these forgotten gifts.

A religious leader, for example, mentors a retired sister in search of a "second career." Fearful that she will be unsuccessful in her search, this older woman questions her decision to resign from teaching. She is frightened by the prospect of job interviews, wonders what additional training she may need, and, at times, regresses and insists that she is incapable of gathering any useful information about those ministries suitable for her.

The provincial can assist this woman by encouraging her during this difficult time. To infantilize her by doing all the necessary work of search and exploration, however, is a betrayal of the mentoring role. To do so would only reinforce the fear of failure already so alive in this woman. Middle-aged mentors need to be guides and supports, not rescuers and saviors. Early in life it is important to have mentors; after midlife, it is essential to be one yourself.

b. Growing Interior Life

Around age forty another aspect of middle adulthood's developmental work gets underway: people feel an increased need to foster their interior life. Even though priesthood and religious life should provide men and women with the structure and time to develop a spiritual life during all the years of adulthood, it is not until midlife that many of them leave the often compulsive, unreflective busyness of their ministries and once more become explorers of the world within.

This journey homeward to oneself usually begins in the middle years and continues throughout the remainder of the life cycle. What sets it in motion? For some people, a spiritual awakening; for others, a growing awareness of personal mortality, or a profound experience of change. Regardless of what initiates this passage, making it is essential for all those who long to be at home with their life of celibate chastity.

c. Integrating our Masculine and Feminine Sides

Men and women are different in a number of ways. For example, Deborah Tannen, a sociolinguist at Georgetown University, points out that many men see life as a struggle to preserve independence and avoid failure; in contrast, a number of women view it as a struggle to preserve intimacy and avoid isolation.

Differences between men and women are often more complicated than they first appear. For example, every person, male and female, has both a masculine and feminine side. A man has an unconscious feminine side; a woman, an unconscious masculine side. To establish relationships of intimacy people need to develop and integrate their masculine and feminine sides. We will discuss this process more fully in Chapter II when exploring the issues of infatuation and intimacy.

Evelyn and James Whitehead point out that early in life we look for ways to "prove ourselves," to have someone or something testify to our identity and worth. Midlife is a time for "finding ourselves"; once we have done so, we discover that there is much less need to prove ourselves. Self-intimacy is the real gift of midlife.

This increased self-knowledge is a key ingredient in the mix we need to grow close to others and to God; the years between the early forties and mid-sixties, then, offer one of the best opportunities for interpersonal and spiritual intimacy to flourish. About midlife, most of us also learn another significant lesson: no matter how much information we acquire about human sexuality, we will never be comfortable with our celibate chastity until we learn what it means to be a spiritual person. Yes, it's that simple.

REFLECTION QUESTIONS

Let's take a few minutes again to reflect on what we've just read. It will be helpful to jot down a few of your reactions to the questions below; put them in the book itself, or in your journal or a notebook. Remember also: it's often helpful to share what you've written with someone else.

1. Midlife is that time in life when most of us face the issue of personal mortality; what's been your experience in that regard?
2. How has your dream found a place in your life at midlife? What have you had to do to make this possible?
3. What impact has midlife had on your understanding

and appreciation of your human sexuality and celibate chastity? Have earlier notions been transformed? If so, what led to the changes?
4. How is your celibate chastity enriching your life in the middle years?
5. What are the rewards and disappointments of this time in your life?

Now let's continue by considering late and late, late adulthood.

D. Late Adulthood

As most people leave middle adulthood, they enter into a period of life evaluation. Knowing they have more years behind them than ahead, these men and women try to determine whether or not they have achieved their life goals. Stated simply, thoughts about death inevitably lead to questions about what it means to have lived. As part of this process of evaluation, people take a look at their past performance and work to resolve conflicts about failures and disappointments. They also begin to prepare for any eventual physical and psychological decline.

This question lies at the heart of anyone's life review: have I lived my life with integrity? The Whiteheads tell us that integrity is the judgment that my life, with all its similarities to the lives of others as well as its idiosyncratic joys and disappointments, could not have been otherwise. It does not deny that I might have regrets or experience guilt about what I have or have not done with my life. Instead, integrity allows me to live in the face of these doubts; it leads to wisdom, an essential strength of character.

Arriving at late adulthood, priests, men and women religious, and others who chose a life of celibate chastity also face a number of sexual challenges; most obviously, they are called to reflect upon the consequences of some earlier choices. Truman Capote's evocative phrase, "Other voices, other rooms," frames their experience; these men and women begin to wonder what their life would have been like if they had not made the choices they did. They also search to discover the ways in which their days have been fruitful.

A woman religious, for example, shares this experience of visiting her family within the past year. "A few weeks before my arrival, my brother rejoiced in the birth of his first grandchild. While the baby was christened during my stay, my brother, unfortunately, was unable to attend; he had suffered a serious heart attack just the previous week.

"On the day of the christening, I stayed with him at the hospital while the rest of the family went to church for the service. On returning, my nephew immediately brought his son into the hospital room and held him close to his own father. My brother held the tiny hand of his grandson with great tenderness; he took it to his lips for a kiss of blessing. I was very moved and thought, what satisfaction for an old man about to leave this life to see the second generation already on its way."

In earlier years, priests and men and women religious shared a similar experience of generativity. They were blessed with the opportunity to pass on the spirit and traditions of their religious family to a new generation; theirs was a sense of continuity.

In our day, however, there are often few, if any younger members with whom to share the heritage of religious life. This loss is felt keenly by many older priests and religious; it leads them to question the worth and purpose of their lives and wonder why it is that a new generation is not forthcoming. Fresh insights into the meaning of the word legacy may help alleviate their distress.

At midlife, we all face this question: Can I, will I, take responsibility for nurturing life? Single, married, man or woman religious, priest — everyone must answer it. The present Church age, however, is forcing priests and men and women religious to see more clearly just who it is they have always nurtured — the next generation of baptized ministers.

Religious congregations were founded for mission not self-preservation; the real legacy of today's sisters, brothers, and priests is what their forebears have always left behind: the next generation of believers, be they lay, ordained, or religious. This broader understanding about the concept of generativity can provide reassurance to many older priests and men and women religious that their lives have been fruitful in ways less obvious than the norm; they too have left a legacy for the future, though not so visible as children and grandchildren.

It is also the old who show the young the adequacy of their culture. The real fear of death is not the loss of one's life but rather the loss of meaning. If a particular life commitment and way of living can support people throughout life and into old age, then the value and significance of both are confirmed. Psychoanalyst Erik Erikson put it this way: healthy children will not fear life if their elders have the integrity not to fear death.

Early adulthood, then, is a time in life for biologically mothering and fathering children. During middle and late adulthood people face a different challenge: they are called upon to emotionally and spiritually nurture subsequent generations. Remember what was said earlier in this chapter: early in life it's important to have mentors; after midlife, it is essential to be one.

E. Late, Late Adulthood

Ninety-year-old playwright George Bernard Shaw had this to say about old age: "Considering the alternative, it feels very good!" As people move into the final years of life, however, physical and mental decline are often more rapid, chronic and catastrophic illness more common, and the death of lifelong friends more frequent. With the onset of their eighties, the majority of people have ceased productive full-time work and lost most of their remaining social roles and status.

What tasks do elderly men and women face as this era of the life cycle gets underway? Coping with impaired health, making adjustments in their living situations so as to provide for any necessary care, dealing with the increasing frequency of death among family members, friends, and relatives.

Living into late, late adulthood, elderly men and women religious, priests, and others who have lived lives of celibate chastity discover that it too is a time for conversion. In dying and letting go of old self-images and understandings, there is also a rising to new ones and greater self-intimacy. Death, closer than at midlife, once again causes them to make some assessments; the meaning of life is clearer. As they complete the developmental work of this period of growth, senior priests, sisters, and brothers discover again one of life's most significant learnings. At the heart of human psychological growth is our faith's central paradox: we need to die in order to rise anew.

Late and late, late adulthood are important times to be at home with our human sexuality and celibate chastity; for the most of us, the developmental work done in these areas during the six or so previous decades continues to bear fruit as our life moves into its senior years. Are there difficulties, though, that older people face when it comes to human sexuality and celibate chastity? Many senior priests and men and women religious cite the death of lifelong friends as one of this period's major hardships. One eighty-two-year old man put it this way: "It's hard to make new friends at my age; I'll never again have friends like the friends I've had. We grew old together; they are gone now and I miss them."

These years between the early sixties and a person's death can span one or a few decades; psychiatrist Carl Jung judged their developmental questions to be chiefly spiritual. Many of us naively enter this period only to learn quickly that the skills and beliefs suitable for an earlier time in life are found wanting after age sixty.

What are the rewards of these two periods? First, having perhaps painfully surrendered a number of myths about ourselves, we discover that mature human and spiritual intimacies are now able to flourish more fully than ever before. Second, having finally faced what it means to be a spiritual person, we are at home, at last, with our life of celibate chastity.

You may have noticed that the eras of the life cycle overlap with one another: even as we are in the process of leaving early adulthood, for example, midlife is already underway. In moving from one era of life to another, we pass through times of transition, periods wherein we evaluate our past and rework important aspects of our life. Some understanding about these often confusing times of change is essential for a fuller appreciation of our growth into mature human sexuality and celibate chastity. Let's turn our attention to them as we conclude this chapter.

LIFE TRANSITIONS

Transitions are times of disorientation and reorientation that mark the turning points on the path of human and spiritual growth. These special times of change begin with an ending; we sense that a chapter of our life is coming to a close. Although we hope earnestly that a new chapter will get underway immediately, the second stage of any life transition usually finds us feeling a bit lost, up-in-the-air, confused, lonely, and alienated. At times like this, we can be sure of only these facts: we cannot go back to where we came from; we are not really sure where we are headed. Psychoanalyst Erik Erikson, quoting a text he once saw hanging over a western bar, summarized our dilemma this way: "I ain't what I ought to be, and I ain't what I'm going to be. But I ain't what I was!"

During the middle phase of any life transition, people often report four unsettling feelings: disengagement, disenchantment, disorientation, loss of identity. To begin with, many men and women find themselves cut off from familiar people, places, and events. Like the character Larry in Eugene O'Neill's play, The *Iceman Cometh*, they are sitting in life's grandstand, observing more than living. While painful, this separation helps us to better confront ourselves and see our relationship with others and God in a new light. Jesus, after all, went into the desert; there he was tempted by power, wealth, and prestige. After forty days, he emerged more deeply aware of his future mission.

Next, a number of people complain about disenchantment during a transition's middle phase. The experience begins with this discovery: to change, we must realize that a significant part of our old world is not real; it is in our head. Author William Bridges points out, for example, that the noble leader, flawless parent, perfect wife, husband or community, and utterly trustworthy friend are an inner cast of characters that we need to surrender.

One final point: most significant life transitions not only include disenchantment in their middle phase, they begin with it.

Does disenchantment have a positive side? Certainly; it helps us mourn those illusions we have about ourselves, our world, and the way it should work. Disenchantment, then, is an important first step in the process of personal and spiritual transformation.

People also lose their familiar roles and self-understandings during the middle of any transition. Those healthy roles we lived out in life, the ones that always made sense, no longer do so. We are just not so sure who we are anymore.

Finally, during these times of life change, most men and

women feel generally disoriented, confused, lost in an unfamiliar world; things that once seemed so important, now no longer matter much. While far from enjoyable, disorientation can be meaningful. Despite its discomfort, this experience helps us become lost enough to find ourselves anew.

The film *On Golden Pond* provides a good illustration of the four unsettling feelings mentioned above. In it, Norman Thayer, Jr., portrayed by Henry Fonda, is having difficulty growing old. He is forgetful, often disoriented, and lacks his former energy.

Norman's old and comfortable roles are gone also. Though retired, he still scans the want ads and even suggests sarcastically that he might follow up on one or two of the job offerings listed. Having shed his old roles Norman feels useless and vulnerable, cut off from his former life.

Finally, this character is disenchanted. All those things he once thought so important and sought after, have now lost their allure. Norman struggles to become someone who is at first unfamiliar to him.

A thirteen-year-old house guest named Billy helps this old man move through his transition. Forgetting to screen the blaze he lit in the hearth, Norman almost sets fire to the house; Billy remarks about the mess created. In response, Norman barks at him, "I guess I'm just not safe to have around anymore."

Ethel, Norman's wife, tries to help Billy understand her husband's situation. She counsels, "Sometimes you have to look hard at a man and realize that he's doing the best he can. He's just trying to find his way." During the middle phase of any life transition that is precisely what most of us are trying to do: find our way. To do so, we need a large dose of patience and compassion, from ourselves and everyone else.

Life transitions come to an end when a new beginning gets under way. While available to everyone, they generally tend to be untidy; new beginnings are the result of an inner realignment of deep longings, values, and motivations.

A religious brother, for example, seeks to change his

ministry. He searches out options and makes an assessment of his talents as well as the needs of his congregation and Church. Getting no hint of a new direction, this man becomes discouraged. Only in surrendering to the emptiness and quiet of his transition's middle stage, does he begin eventually to pick up some subtle signals: the comments of a friend, an opportunity offered unexpectedly, and some inner promptings move him toward a new and rewarding beginning.

In making any new beginning, keep these points in mind. First of all, when the time is right for change, stop getting ready to act and act! Don't be like a person in therapy who enjoys collecting insights but demonstrates little interest in behavioral change. Stated simply, just do it.

Next, identify with the final results of your new beginning. Be it changing residences, ending a relationship, or beginning a new phase in life, think of yourself as moving in that direction. Also, do not become preoccupied with immediate results; concentrate on the process of meeting your goal rather than the goal itself. Finally, always remember: you cannot rush a new beginning. When the time is right for it to start, you'll know it.

Why are transitional experiences so important to our discussion? Questions about sexuality, intimacy, and celibate chastity most often come to the fore during these times of life change. Those earlier questions about personal identity and intimacy — What am I doing with my life? Is it possible for me to live in a way that best combines my talents, current desires, values, and aspirations? What do I truly get from and give to others? Does anyone really care about me? Do I really care about anyone else? — all come front and center during the middle stage of any life transition.

As we leave this first chapter, pay heed to its key points: our definitions of human sexuality and intimacy are much wider than genital sexual behavior; celibate chastity is one of a number of ways in which to be a sexual person; our experience of human sexuality and celibate chastity is colored by our age and life circumstances; life transitions are important times of change over the course of life.

In our next chapter we will explore two issues: personal identity and intimacy. While men and women come to an awareness of identity and mature intimacy in different ways, a clear understanding of both is necessary to achieve a deeper appreciation of the complexity and richness of human sexuality and celibate chastity. Let's begin on that note.

REFLECTION QUESTIONS

As we come to the end of this chapter, let's spend a few minutes reflecting on late and late, late adulthood and also times of transition. Keep a pencil or pen handy to jot down a few of your thoughts in response to the questions below. Remember, sharing your ideas with others most often enriches your time of reflection.

1. What challenges have you faced (or think you will face) as you move(d) into late and late, late adulthood? How have these demands shaped you?
2. Think about your lifelong friends, those who have companioned you for years. Have you lost any to death in late and late, late adulthood? What effect has their absence had on you?
3. What personal challenges have you faced (or expect to face) in late and late, late adulthood regarding sexuality and celibate chastity? Looking back on your life, how has celibate chastity enriched your life?
4. Spend time describing a period of transition in your life. Can you identify the feelings of disengagement, disorientation, disillusionment, and loss of identity? What most helped you cope as you moved through the transition's phases?

REFERENCES

Bridges, William. *Transitions*. (Reading, MA: Addison-Wesley, 1980).

Jung, Carl. *Modern Man in Search of a Soul*, trans. W.S. Dell and Cary F. Baynes (New York, NY: Harcourt, Brace and World, 1933).

Levinson, Daniel J. *Seasons of a Man's Life*. (New York, NY: Alfred A. Knopf, 1978).

Nelson, James. *Embodiment: An Approach to Sexuality and Christian Theology*. (Minneapolis, MN: Augsburg, 1978).

Sammon, Sean D. *Growing Pains in Ministry*. (Mystic, CT: Twenty-Third Publications, 1983).

Sammon, Sean D. "Planning for the Third Age," *Church Personnel Issues*. (National Association of Church Personnel Administrators) August 1992, pp. 1-7.

Sellner, Edward C. *Mentoring: The Ministry of Spiritual Kinship*. (Notre Dame, IN: Ave Maria Press, 1990).

Tannen, Deborah. *You Just Don't Understand*. (New York, NY: Ballantine Books, 1990).

Whitehead, Evelyn E. and James D. *Christian Life Patterns*. (New York, NY: Doubleday, 1979).

Whitehead, Evelyn E. and James D. *Seasons of Strength*. (New York, NY: Doubleday, 1984).

Chapter II

TWO SIDES OF THE SAME COIN: IDENTITY AND INTIMACY

Another story!

This one's about an elderly pastor who had served his parish in that position for more than twenty-five years. The old man felt stagnant, "stuck in a rut." He knew he needed a change; something, almost anything, that would get his life moving once again.

As the elderly pastor thought about his dilemma, he struck on this idea: why not ask for a transfer to another parish? Surely, thought the old man, a "geographical cure" would get his life moving again.

The pastor went to the phone to call his Bishop; as he was about to dial, however, he remembered that since the Second Vatican Council there had been a personnel board in this diocese. Now, the old man did not believe much in personnel boards but he knew it was the route he must take if he wanted his transfer. He called the Board's chair and made an appointment for the following week.

The elderly pastor arrived promptly for his meeting and explained his plight to the Board members. He pointed out that he was stuck in a rut and needed a change. He told the Board members that he had visited every family in the parish about as often as he would care to see them, and, he believed, just about as often as they cared to see him! Without doubt, at least in the elderly pastor's mind, it was time to move on.

The Board members heard the old man out; they were quite sympathetic. But this group had a piece of information that the elderly pastor lacked: there was a shortage of men to serve as pastors in this diocese. If the Board transferred him, it had no one with whom to replace him. So, what did the Board members do? They "sweet-talked" the old man. The Board's chair said, "Don't be foolish, Father, you have done a wonderful job in that parish; people love you, they respect your leadership," and so forth.

The elderly pastor grew uneasy, fearing he would not be granted the transfer he requested. So, he said to the Board members, "You know, there is something I forgot to mention: I do get a lot of complaints, well, not really complaints, more some expressions of concern about the quality of my homilies." The Board members had heard some rumblings about the quality of this man's homilies, but with no replacement for the old pastor, they told him they were unable to help.

The elderly pastor thanked the Board members for their time, went home, and said to himself, "I knew these boards were a waste of time!" He called the Bishop immediately and made an appointment for the following week.

The Bishop was as gracious as the Board members had been; he heard the pastor out and was sympathetic to his concerns. The Bishop, however, also had that piece of information that the Board had and the pastor didn't: because of the shortage of men to serve as pastors, if he removed the old man there would be no one with whom to replace him.

What did the Bishop do? Exactly what the Board members had done; he "sweet-talked" the elderly pastor. Listening to the Bishop, the old man grew increasingly concerned; so, he blurted out, "Bishop, I forgot to mention that I do get a number of complaints about my homilies!"

If anyone in the diocese had heard about the quality of this priest's homilies, it was the Bishop. So he said to the elderly pastor, "Well, Father, that is an area of concern; however, rather than transfer you, why don't I just give you a few pointers from my own experience that might help you with your sermons."

The Bishop then went on to relate that just the previous Sunday, at the time of the homily, he had climbed the steps of the pulpit in the Cathedral and said to the congregation assembled, "I have an announcement!" He continued by saying that since he rarely made announcements at the time of the homily, a number of people looked up to see what he had to say.

He went on, "Yes, I have an announcement, a very important announcement: I'm in love." With that said, just about everyone in the church looked up from what they were reading or stopped what they were doing.

The Bishop then went on to say,"Yes, I'm in love, I'm in love with a very beautiful woman; her name is Mary, the mother of God." With that said, since it was the month of May, he delivered a homily about Mary, the mother of God.

The old man thanked the Bishop for his time, took his leave, and went home. By this time he was desperate. Racking his brains, he wondered just how he could get out of this parish. Then he had an idea!

The very next Sunday, at the time of the homily, the elderly pastor climbed the steps of the pulpit in his parish church, looked out at the crowd, and said in a clear, loud voice, "I have an announcement!" Since this man rarely said much of interest at the time of the homily, a number of people looked up from what they were reading to see what he had to say.

The old man said, "Yes, I have an announcement, a very important announcement: the bishop is in love!" The line was a show stopper; everyone in the church put down what they were reading and waited for the elderly pastor to go on. He continued, "Yes, the bishop is in love; he's in

> love with a very beautiful woman, but for the life of me, I cannot remember her name." The old man got his transfer!

You might wonder: doesn't the story above better illustrate an ingenious or "difficult" person than the themes of identity and intimacy to be discussed in this chapter. Let me stretch its meaning, however, and say that the shock and interest of the two congregations always perplex me; those assembled in the cathedral and the old priest's parish church are stunned on hearing that the bishop is in love.

Conventional wisdom assures us that "falling in love" is just not part of the life script of most sisters, priests, or brothers. It often goes a step farther and implies that there is little place for intimacy in religious life or priesthood. Nothing could be further from the truth. Let's look at why this is so.

Although this chapter is divided into six parts, we'll see time and again that identity and intimacy go hand in hand; one is an essential part of the other. For example, for most men, mature intimacy is not possible without a sense of personal identity. Unless he is at home with himself, a man just doesn't get close to others. A man who is unsure of himself might feel the need to present an image of extraordinary competence to his friends and colleagues; he is, however, unable to share with them any of his weaknesses, needs, or insecurities.

Women, in contrast, form their sense of identity through relationships; in relationship, a woman comes to discover who she is. Connection and relationship are important to women, separation and autonomy preoccupy men. While men and women come to it in different ways, then, a healthy sense of personal identity is an essential ingredient for both in any relationship of intimacy.

A number of women in religious life, however, may, at times, identify with some of what will be said about male identity formation. Prior to Vatican II, programs of religious formation were often insensitive to gender differences; those used by women's congregations were frequently modeled on programs created for men. As a consequence, many sisters were forced into a mold of development more appropriate for men than women.

The six major headings in this chapter are entitled identity, intimacy, the masculine and feminine: friendship between men and women, signs of failure to arrive at mature intimacy, barriers to intimacy, and some "second thoughts." Under the first, we'll describe the process of forming an identity; we'll also say a word about the ways in which identity changes over the course of life.

Second, we'll define the word intimacy and describe the elements needed for any relationship of mature intimacy. Third, we'll talk about the masculine and feminine sides of each of us and the roles they play in relationships between men and women.

Fourth, we'll identify some of the signs of failure to arrive at mature intimacy and provide examples to illustrate each of them. Fifth, we'll point to some barriers to intimacy and discuss the effect that growing up in a troubled family can have on our adult relationships.

As we close, we'll report on Sheila Murphy's recent work investigating intimacy among priests, sisters, and brothers.

A final note as we begin. A healthy sense of identity and relationships of mature intimacy are as important for people living a life of celibate chastity as they are for everyone else. With that thought in mind, let's get underway.

IDENTITY

Personal identity answers the question: "Who am I?" During the late teen years, everyone is called upon to form some sort of initial adult identity: that feeling of knowing who you are and where you are going. Identity, however, is never purchased cheaply. To achieve one, we must be willing to do three things: explore options for living; experience confusion and any crises that may follow; eventually, make choices and commitments.

A. Forming an Identity

What are the experiences of exploration, confusion and crisis, choice and commitment like? Consider this simple example. With twenty-five dollars to spend and no more, you set out to buy a shirt. Entering a department store, you spy one that you like; after examining it, you look at the price tag: twenty-five dollars. You move on and another attractive shirt catches your eye. Its price? Also, twenty-five dollars. You find still another one, equally attractive; its price: the same as the other two.

Since you have only twenty-five dollars to spend, the more you explore in this store, the greater will be your confusion or crisis of choice. Eventually, though, you will have to choose one shirt from among a number of attractive options. While this choice, and the commitment it entails, will be difficult, you must make it to complete the task you set out to accomplish.

Forming an identity is much the same. We spend time looking at our options for living and exploring various paths in life to follow. Many adolescents find themselves in this dilemma; they experiment, in fantasy, with a variety of careers and relationships. On Monday, for example, a fifteen-year-old boy plans to be a chemist; by the following Thursday, the field of medicine is more attractive to him.

Confusion and crises follow naturally after exploration. These words refer to those periods of struggle and questioning, throughout the course of life, during which we re-think old roles and life plans. Finally, in forming an identity, a time comes when we must make some choices about the meaning and direction of our life; the word commitment is used to describe our investment in what we have chosen.

B. Identity Formation among Priests and Men and Women Religious

Many men and women in formation for religious and priestly life also experience times of exploration, and confusion and crisis. For example, a number of young professed religious and newly ordained priests fall in love. They wonder seriously whether or not to pursue a particular love relationship rather than their recent life choice. Whenever people explore other options for living, they will almost inevitably experience confusion and crisis. Whatever they decide, their struggle helps them form an identity.

C. Foreclosing Identity

What about people who skip the exploration and crisis stages of identity formation: those who jump into a life commitment, hoping that it will tell them who they are. These men and women foreclose their identity; the results of this decision are disappointing.

Some people, for example, afraid of sexuality or unsure of their life's purpose, look to marriage, priesthood, or religious life for an answer. They hope that one of these life choices will allay their fears and answer their concerns. It just doesn't work that way. Foreclosing identity is similar to ordering a suit of clothes through the mail; it never fits right! The jacket is always a bit too tight; the skirt too short. Not tailor-made for the person, the suit looks as though it belongs to someone else. Foreclosed identities appear much the same.

What do those who foreclose identity look like? Usually stable, sober, and responsible; they are also somewhat passive, lacking curiosity and a sense of independence. Their relationships with others are often stereotyped: they are more at home relating through a role than person to person.

People who foreclose their identity commit themselves too early. Failing to explore their options for living, they refuse to question their values and goals. Instead, they commit themselves because of external circumstances or to please an authority like parents, an older priest, or a former teacher. These men and women make a dangerous decision; later in life it exacts a cost.

D. Identity Throughout the Course of Life

Suppose I foreclose my identity early in life; does that decision condemn me to years of walking around with hunched shoulders bemoaning the fact that I am a foreclosed identity? Not really. Although it appears, first of all, during the adolescent years, an identity "crisis" can re-occur during any period of life transition. Remember those questions mentioned in Chapter I — What am I doing with my life? Is it possible for me to live in a way that best combines my talents, current desires, values and aspirations? What do I truly get from and give to others? Does anyone really care about me? Do I really care about anyone else? — all play a central role in any process of identity re-formulation.

In the midst of change and transition, we re-evaluate our commitments, explore alternative ways to live out our life, and move toward building a new identity, one that will serve us well during the years ahead. Novelist John Updike's fictional character, Tom Marshfield, for example, began one of his life transitions with this question: "Who am I?" Searching his face in the mirror, he said, "I do not recognize it as mine. It no more fits my inner light than the shade of a bridge lamp fits its bulb."

During early adulthood, we wonder who we are becoming; later in life, most of us question who we have become. This second task is more difficult for those who foreclosed identity early in life. During those times of transition mentioned in Chapter I, these men and women are highly vulnerable to a crisis of identity. While some embrace it, many more demand that their environment remain constant and consistently supportive. Lacking such an environment, they are thrown into distress; panic and intense self-questioning ensue. For some who foreclosed previously, this experience helps them achieve a new identity. Others, however, shed one foreclosed identity only to hastily take up another.

A number of men and women religious and priests reading this book probably entered religious and priestly life during their late teens. Consequently, they gave themselves little opportunity to explore other options for living. Does this fact suggest that they live with a foreclosed identity? Not necessarily.

Success in the task of achieving an identity does not appear related to age of commitment; rather, it is one's life experiences that are important. Some people enter seminary and religious formation late in life and still have a foreclosed identity. Remember that the essential ingredients for healthy identity formation are exploration, confusion and crisis, and choice making and commitment. If the first two are missing at any age, the risk of foreclosing is high. A genuine identity helps us enter society with confidence and assume our responsibilities as an adult. As mentioned earlier, it also plays a central role in the next topic we will discuss: intimacy.

REFLECTION QUESTIONS

Once again, take a few moments to reflect quietly on what you've just read. Have a pen or pencil and some paper handy to make a few notes. Also, remember that sharing your reflections with others can enrich them even more.

1. How would you reply if someone asked you this question, "Who are you and where are you going in life?" As you respond, recall the price you paid to answer this question in the first place; remember also those times, later in life, when you had to rework your reply. Spend some time considering the options you explored, any confusion and crises you weathered, the choices you made to arrive at an answer. Jot down a few notes about each of these areas.
2. Was there ever a time in your life when you foreclosed identity? If so, what made you foreclose? How did you deal with the challenge of reworking your foreclosed identity?

INTIMACY

James and Evelyn Whitehead frame their definition of intimacy as a question: Am I sure enough of myself and confident enough of my ability that I can risk being influenced through closeness with someone else? Think about that notion for a moment. The connection between identity and intimacy is clear: unless I am at home with myself, closeness with another will frighten or overwhelm me.

The Whiteheads' definition suggests also that intimacy requires some risk of self-understanding; the way in which I define myself, my identity, can be stretched in a close relationship. Psychoanalyst Erik Erikson emphasizes the same point: to move from the adolescent years into early adulthood, men and women need to risk their self-definition. They must allow others to come close to them in such a way that they can be known, influenced, and possibly changed as a result of the relationship.

Many situations call for the risk of my self-definition; let's take a closer look at some of them.

A. Close Friendships

Without some risk of self-definition, any relationship will die eventually. Close friendships are no exception to this rule. Perhaps even more than other relationships, they challenge me to risk my self-understanding.

Mature friendship allows me to relax the well-guarded stance with which I usually face the world and most other people. As a consequence, friends reach a part of me that is inaccessible to others; they know me as others do not.

With a friend I am also better able to risk stretching the boundaries of my self-understanding; I can raise questions about my self-definition. For example, a friend is not frightened by my weaknesses—I can share my fears, concerns, difficulties; as a consequence, I learn to be a bit more at home with them myself.

People who refuse to risk their self-definition discover that their friendships fail to flourish. Without doubt, intimacy with all it entails, is at the heart of mature friendship.

B. Group Membership

Many communities have one or two members who live on the fringes of the group. These men and women move in and out of the community's life but refuse to let the other members have any claim on them. For example, if the group talks about participating together in a weekend activity, "fringe" members will encourage the others to make their plans, adding that they will fit in if they are able.

For most of us, absence from community activities and full participation in the life of the group occurs from time to time;

for "fringe" people, it's a way of life. These men and women have difficulty with intimacy; they refuse to allow the group to come close enough to them so they could possibly be changed by it. They pay a terrible price in protecting their self-definition: they keep the community at arm's length and manage only to maintain their isolation. Theirs is a pseudo-intimacy: in reality, these people live alone in the midst of the group.

c. Sexual Encounters

In the life of a number of married people, mature genital love is not reached easily or quickly. Erik Erikson, for example, points out that, early on, much of the sexual life can be self-seeking.

The Whiteheads, though, observe that rituals of lovemaking and the experience of orgasm highlight features common to other experiences of intimacy: the impulse to share oneself with another, the anxiety that usually surrounds a moment of self-revelation, acceptance, and the give-and-take of mutuality. For a marriage to work and sexual union to be fulfilling, those involved must risk being influenced through closeness with each other.

Heterosexual marriage, however, is not the only genital context for risking self-definition. Ongoing discussion about stable homosexual unions needs to continue so that we can better understand the challenges of intimacy faced by a number of gay men and lesbian women. The experiences of many single people and those called to a life of celibate chastity also suggest that the development of intimacy does not always involve sexual union or genital expression.

d. Cooperation and Competition

In all of the examples mentioned thus far, we see that along with self-disclosure, vulnerability and mutuality are central aspects of any relationship of intimacy. They are also essential ingredients in the tasks of cooperation and competition. Consider this example: you are asked to work on an important project as a member of an ad-hoc team. For the group to be successful, what will be required of each team member? One, a willingness to share thoughts, ideas, and feelings; two, an agreement that it's OK to be uncertain or wrong; three, a mutual respect among the team members.

The experience of cooperation and competition also helps us stretch our self-understanding. Working with others on a task, we become aware of personal gifts and abilities not recognized previously. One woman, for example discovers she can skillfully facilitate a group and, thus, expedite an assigned task. So also, many athletes, playing the season's most challenging game, often discover previously unknown talents and endurance as they give their all to win.

Mature cooperation and competition, then, can stretch our self-understanding and change us. This outcome, though, is not surprising; after all, self-disclosure, vulnerability, and mutuality are at the heart of these experiences. People who cooperate and compete allow themselves to be influenced by others; they risk the type of closeness called for in any relationship of intimacy.

E. Prayer

Some people talk about a "God of surprises"; many of us, however, are a bit afraid of such a God. We prefer to keep God at arm's length and are more at home with a predictable God, one who won't disturb our well made plans.

In recent years, for example, the meaning of the word discernment has often been misunderstood. Discernment entails a process of coming to know what's in the heart of God for me; if I pray regularly and enjoy intimacy with God, often enough God's desire ends up being my desire.

Some of us, however, approach discernment in this way: we make up God's mind to serve our own purpose. For example, asked by our community to take on a new assignment, we promise to pray over the request. In reality, though, we refuse to talk with God about our mixed feelings, our fears, and God's and our heart's desire. Authentic discernment demands that I risk intimacy with God, a closeness that could, in the long run, change my self-definition and my life.

Most people will agree that the five examples given above illustrate situations where the need to risk one's self-definition is clear. As a reader, though, you might be asking yourself some additional questions: if intimacy with others takes time and energy, with just how many people can I expect to be intimate? Do I need to be intimate with everyone with whom I live? After all, I don't even like some of them! Let's explore the topic of mature intimacy; our discussion of this issue may provide answers to some of these questions.

MATURE INTIMACY

Mature intimacy includes two elements: I feel drawn toward self-disclosure and empathy; at the same time, I am held back by caution and selectivity. Let's take a look at these two polar opposites.

A. Self-disclosure and Empathy

What do we mean by the term self-disclosure? Sharing with another something important about myself. Some people have more difficulty with self-disclosure than others; it is, however, an important part of mature intimacy and one with which many of us are familiar.

With that said, we must realize that there is also such a thing as too much self-disclosure. Consider this example: you are at a party when a total stranger comes up to you and begins to share in great detail his or her life story. What is your reaction? Most of us want to back off and tell the other person we are not really interested in hearing more.

Social convention, however, often leads us to excuse ourselves for a moment to get something to drink or eat. As we make our journey to the bar or serving table, we also hope fervently that someone else will move into the spot we just vacated. Returning with that drink or a plate of food in hand, we are not surprised to find our former conversation partner now telling another perfect stranger about the intimate details of his or her life.

This example illustrates the fact that self-disclosure does not necessarily equal mature intimacy. Relationships take time; some parts of myself, shared easily in certain relationships, often could not have been spoken about earlier.

People, though, often confuse self-disclosure and empathy with mature intimacy. During the late 1960's and early 1970's, for example, encounter or T-groups were popular. These gatherings consisted of six to ten strangers who came together for one or several days to practice the skill of self-disclosure and experience empathy. For many people, this type of group was useful; it helped them experience their emotional life and share it with others.

Not everyone, however, benefited from an encounter or T-group. One middle-aged woman, for example, had this to say at the end of her experience: "Never have I been with so few people, for so long a time, come to know them so well and dislike them so thoroughly!"

The interaction of an encounter or T-group was often confused with the experience of intimacy. Some people returned home euphoric from their weekend session only to find that their spouse, roommate, friends, or fellow community members could not identify with their experience. Some just graduated T-group members then accused others of a lack of understanding about intimacy. This allegation was uncalled for; those who participate in a T-group may learn a great deal about self-disclosure and empathy. However, because such groups usually fail to insure some continuity of relationship among their members, participants do not necessarily increase their experience of mature intimacy.

B. Caution and Selectivity

Mature intimacy, however, also has another side to it: caution and selectivity. The vast majority of us, for example, probably found it difficult to identify with the guest at the party mentioned earlier, the one who spent the evening telling his or her life story to a procession of strangers. Most of us feel a tug of caution when involved in a relationship; we don't share our inner world with everyone.

Psychologist Lillian Rubin defines friends as reliable emotional confidants. They are, first of all, people with whom we share confidences. Friends, though, have to be more than confidants; they must be linked together emotionally and enjoy each other's inner world.

Over time, a history also develops between two friends; they prove themselves dependable, one to the other. When friends reach this point in their relationship, they realize that they are valued before ever being evaluated; they have become reliable emotional confidants.

In the best of friendships, however, there are times when one or the other feels held back; even a best friend doesn't necessarily know everything about you. Caution and selectivity, then, are normal and necessary aspects of mature intimacy.

Is there such a thing as too much caution or selectivity in a relationship? Absolutely! Some people are so cautious and selective that they never reveal much of themselves to anyone. These men and women end up as isolates; they might live in a community or family, but no one really knows who they are.

What is the bottom line on mature intimacy? Don't be surprised to experience the push and pull of these two elements: being drawn toward self-disclosure and empathy; being held back due to caution and selectivity.

REFLECTION QUESTIONS

1. Spend some time thinking about the people with whom you are closest these days; name them, one by one, recalling all the while the history of your relationship together — when did it start; what drew you together; how has the friendship deepened over time? In what ways have you risked closeness with these special people in your life? Think of a symbol that captures the heart of these intimate relationships — an image, a poem, the words of a song, a painting, etc. — a symbol that captures the heart of these friendships.

THE MASCULINE/FEMININE: FRIENDSHIP BETWEEN MEN AND WOMEN

Psychologist Carol Gilligan puts differences between men and women into perspective with this comment: "It all goes back, of course, to Adam and Eve; a story that shows, among other things, that if you make a woman out of a man, you are bound to get into trouble."

Men and women differ in a number of ways. As mentioned earlier, women often focus on the interdependence among people. Men, in contrast, frequently center their attention on autonomy and self-fulfillment; care on the part of others can be experienced as interference.

Every person, however, is also androgynous, having both masculine and feminine sides. Among women, the masculine side is often unconscious; the same is true of many a man's feminine side. To establish a relationship of mature intimacy, the masculine and feminine aspects of both persons involved must achieve a certain level of integration.

If people are androgynous, why has this fact eluded us for so many years? Jungian analyst and Episcopal priest John Sanford cites a number of reasons. First of all, some of us give little importance to self-knowledge. Faced with emotional confusion and pain, for example, some people still choose to live meaningless lives rather than come to know themselves better.

Next, some aspects of ourselves defy greater self-knowledge. These shadow traits, often obvious to others, are hidden from us. Two examples illustrate this point. One, the gospel story about a man who saw the splinter in his neighbor's eye but failed to see the beam in his own. Two, those situations where you have complained to a friend about the behavior of another only to have your friend say, "I'm surprised that her behavior upsets you so. After all, you do the same thing yourself!" The principle is the same here: even though our shadow side is apparent to everyone else, we are often the last to know about it.

Finally, we lack knowledge about our unconscious feminine or masculine side because we typically project it onto others; as a result, we judge that the qualities associated with it belong to another and have little to do with us.

A. Integration

There are many reasons to integrate one's feminine and masculine sides. To begin with, doing so helps us understand better the origin of sexual stereotypes; it also helps us discard these distorted images of what a man or woman should be.

The terms masculine and feminine refer to the meaning of

gender, not to biological gender, that is male and female. Every culture has its gender images. In ours, for example, little boys are taught not to cry; young girls are often cautioned against becoming tomboys. Rigid adherence to gender images is quite problematic: it leads to skewed emotional development and difficulties with intimacy.

A second good reason for working toward the integration of my masculine and feminine sides — to enhance the possibility of intimacy in my life — is central to our discussion. Midlife is a good time for doing some serious work in this area.

Why so late in life, you might ask? The reasons are simple. During early adulthood, many men are frightened by their feminine side. Women also have their difficulties: most of them don't want to be thought of as too masculine. A young woman, for example, may shy away from expressing her natural assertiveness and competence because her masculine side is too threatening; at the same time, a young man fears the implications of his more intuitive feminine qualities.

During their twenties and thirties, then, men and women struggle with intimacy in different ways. A man often sees a danger in closeness; he fears it will limit his independence. In contrast, a young woman battles with fears of abandonment; she is apprehensive about separation.

When some men get close to a woman, their sense of masculinity is threatened. Scared by intimacy, they move away. At the same time, the young woman, threatened by separation, moves closer. In novice adulthood, while a number of men are having difficulty with their relationships, many women are finding it hard to separate and become an individual.

What effect does midlife have on this situation? A profound one. Awareness of personal mortality causes us to be less concerned about the demands of gender images. Prior to this time in life, for example, many men keep an emotional distance from women because they remind them of their unconscious feminine side. This situation begins to change about the late thirties and early forties. Along the same line, a woman in novice adulthood may define herself solely through her relationships; to stand alone is frightening because it forces her to come face to face with her masculine side. For this woman also, a growing awareness of personal mortality can be a turning point.

B. Projection

Because our unconscious masculine or feminine side presents a threat to us, we often project its traits onto others. Projecting some aspect of myself makes it look as though it belongs to another and has little to do with me. Consider the example of an overhead projector and screen. The transparency containing the information we plan to present is set on a projector; resting on top, it looks as though it were part of the machine. Once the overhead is turned on, however, the material on the transparency gets projected onto the screen. Although it now looks as though it is part of the screen, the transparency with its information still rests on the projector.

When we project something of our unconscious masculine or feminine side onto another, that person becomes greatly overvalued or undervalued. Sanford, for example, points out that when the positive aspects of a man's feminine side are projected onto a woman, she becomes highly desirable to him — the object of his erotic fantasies and sexual longings. He believes that he would be fulfilled if only he made love to her.

This situation becomes, in time, suffocating for many women. As she works in the relationship to develop her own personality, she finds that this same man now begins to project negative parts of his unconscious feminine side onto her. He starts to blame her for his unhappiness and negative moods. Should we be surprised? Not really; after all, this man has been relating to his projection, not to a real person.

In contrast, Sanford points out that when a woman projects her unconscious masculine side onto a man, she sees him as a savior, guide, and hero; she comes to believe that only through him can she be complete. Over time, however, she begins to project the negative aspects of her unconscious masculine side onto this man: her earlier savior and guide is transformed into an infuriating and frustrating man responsible for all her feelings of belittlement and disappointment.

c. Projection Produces Infatuation

Projection, as described above, has very little to do with intimacy. Instead, it produces a state of mutual fascination and infatuation. As valuable a prelude as this state can be to emotional growth and mature intimacy, relationships founded solely on infatuation do not last; to the extent that my relationships are built on projection, I am actually in love with some aspects of myself.

Real love occurs between real people, not projections. Falling in love, or infatuation, is merely a step toward intimacy. The latter is only possible, however, when the former dissolves. Mature intimacy requires that people take responsibility for their happiness or unhappiness; no longer can they expect another to make them happy nor can they blame that person for their bad moods, frustrations, or problems.

d. Integration at Midlife

In midlife, many men, through a relationship, discover the importance of intimacy and care about others. This knowledge is something that a number of women may have come to earlier in life. Likewise, many midlife women, in their relationships, stop trying to be selfless in a self-destructive manner. Early in life, they may have judged themselves by their ability to care for others. At midlife, they have second thoughts about this notion that the way to sustain a relationship is to take care of other people. A number, instead, talk directly to others about what they need and want. Each of these women starts to realize that one of the people it's important not to hurt is herself.

E. Failing to Integrate the Masculine and Feminine

A failure to integrate my masculine and feminine sides gives rise to several consequences. Sanford remarks that a man who is out of touch with his unconscious feminine side appears sulky, overly sensitive, and withdrawn; he acts peevish and depressed and is unavailable for relationship.

Such a man's speech is also often peppered with sarcasm, innuendo, and poisonous jabs that sometimes pass for humor. What is the origin of this behavior? One, the man's work may drain him, leaving little room for his emotional life. Two, he might have difficulty expressing his feelings; consequently, they fall into his unconscious and end up getting expressed indirectly in moodiness and covert hostile actions.

If a man's unconscious feminine side is the master of his moods, a woman's unconscious masculine side is the champion of her opinions. It reflects itself in the shoulds and oughts of her critics' committee.

The negative aspects of a woman's unconscious masculine side include judgments, critical statements, and generalizations that do not spring from her own process of thinking and feeling. Rather, they have been picked up from various authoritative sources: parents, her Church, religious superiors, and books and articles. If these negative aspects get projected onto others, we have a woman who is judged to be blunt and hypercritical. She pays a terrible price: the loss of her creativity and a growing belief that she has little to offer others.

We all need to increase in our lives the possibility of intimacy with others. As we come to accept our masculine and feminine sides, we grow in our ability for genuine closeness. Every relationship calls for a balance between individuality and togetherness; to work at integrating our masculine and feminine sides leads ultimately to greater self-knowledge and acceptance.

FRIENDSHIPS BETWEEN MEN AND WOMEN

We've said it before, but it bears repeating: when it comes to relationships, men and women have differences in style and expectation. As mentioned earlier, men friends do things together; women talk things over. Let's explore each of these points more fully.

Michael McGill, Professor of Organizational Behavior and Administration at Southern Methodist University, suggests that men usually come together around something; the bonds they develop have more to do with solidarity than with self-disclosure. Early in life, for example, men learn how to be part of a team. In adulthood, team work continues to be important for them, on the job or when they get together to work out, or to play golf or tennis. It's the things that men do together that bind them; often enough, if you take away those things, many men stop coming together.

Women are different. Their relationships with other women are often more important than anything they might do together. Lillian Rubin, for example reminds us that women value their friendships with other women especially for the emotional support and understanding they receive; they tend to spend their time with other women exploring their personal experience and inner world of meaning.

To illustrate the differences between men and women in the areas of self-disclosure and relationships, McGill provides this striking example. If a woman calls a woman and says, "Let's go to lunch," the other woman usually replies, "When?" If a man calls another man, however, and says, "Let's go to lunch," the response is most likely to be, "Why?"

The clear differences between men and women are also obvious in the friendships they form with one another; expectations about emotional sharing and sexual attraction can easily lead to confusion. How do people report their experiences in these situations? Some men indicate that they sometimes feel pressured by a woman friend to reveal more of themselves than is comfortable for them. For example, one man reported that his friend often said to him: "We never talk." His response, "OK, what do you want to talk about?" always seemed to be somewhat less than helpful to her.

In contrast, many women report disappointment that their male friends are not so forthcoming in terms of emotional sharing as they would like them to be. Such a woman might find herself saying to a man, "I never know what's going on with you."

Men and women, though, agree strongly on this point: in cross-gender relationships, the issue of sex has to be resolved before the friendship can deepen. If a man or woman, feeling strong sexual attraction in such a relationship, fails to talk about his or her feelings with the other, real trouble lies ahead.

With all this said, it is important to emphasize, once again, some of the fruits of mature friendship. First of all, with friends we don't always have to be consistent; we can think and feel differently on alternate days with little consequence. Also, while friendship is not therapy, it does have a therapeutic aspect: it is often critical during periods of significant personal change when our hopes and goals may put us at odds with the way things are "supposed to be."

REFLECTION QUESTIONS

1. Take some time to think about a relationship you've had with a member of the opposite sex. What was satisfying about it? What differences in expectation and style led to confusion between the two of you? What do you value most about your relationships with members of the opposite sex?
2. Think about a time in your life when you were infatuated. Describe the experience — its feelings and what ran through your mind. What did you learn from the experience of infatuation?

SIGNS OF A FAILURE TO ARRIVE AT MATURE INTIMACY

A failure to arrive at mature intimacy usually results in some type of avoidance. Some examples of this outcome? To begin with, men and women in trouble with intimacy often suffer from isolation. It differs from solitude and has little to do with people who savor time alone or enjoy their own company on occasion. Those who choose isolation sense they have to remain alone; coming close to others is experienced as dangerous.

Stereotyped behavior is a second example of a failure to arrive at mature intimacy. The term describes a situation where a person feels more at home relating through a role rather than person to person.

Roles are important; it's their overuse that creates difficulty. As guests at a party, for example, we often find it helpful to know that other party-goers share something in common with us. Teachers tend to have a lot in common with other teachers; so also, homemakers share many of the same experiences and difficulties. Knowing that someone shares a similar day-to-day role often helps oil the interaction that is central to any social gathering.

Other people also expect us to live out our designated roles. If you consult with a doctor, you are most interested usually in stating your physical complaint, getting a thorough examination and accurate diagnosis, and receiving any necessary medication and medical advice. The vast majority of people who visit doctors are not particularly interested in their physician's personal life.

Suppose that you work as a counselor; a young man comes for an appointment and shares with you something of his emotional difficulties. This young man expects you to help him. He won't find it very beneficial if you step out of your role and respond to his tale:"You think you have problems; you should have my life!"

The overuse of a role, though, can lead to difficulties. An example? Have you ever lived with a community member who is taking her first graduate level counseling course? One sunny Saturday morning, you are sitting in the dining room having breakfast and dreaming about ways in which you can enjoy the day. As our first year graduate student moves through the dining room en route to her morning class, you say to her, "Nice day, isn't it?" She pauses, looks at you, and says: "Tell me more about that." Now, that is the overuse of a role!

The overuse of a role keeps others at a distance. A teacher who spends the dinner hour giving mini-lessons to everyone else around the table may teach them a great deal. Chances are, however, they will never find out much about the person delivering the lectures. The same holds true for a counselor who spends time at every social gathering she attends listening to the problems of others. In shedding our roles at appropriate times, we allow others to come close to us in a way that can influence us.

Promiscuity is a final example of a failure to arrive at mature intimacy. We need to be careful about how we define this term. The Whiteheads have this to say about the topic: promiscuity is the hectic seeking after intimacy in improbable relationships where circumstances are such that I cannot share or reveal much about myself. Let's examine this definition more closely.

When most people hear the word promiscuity, something like a "one-night stand" comes to mind. The term does include ideas like that; it also includes a great deal more. Take a religious brother, for example, whose ministry is high school teaching. This man spends all his time with students. If his community plans a social on Tuesday night, he already has a student government meeting scheduled. He can't attend that weekend day of recollection the group talked about last week because he's working the junior retreat.

Don't even think about trying to plan with him for a month ahead; almost every waking minute he has is scheduled to be with the students. If, in exasperation, you ask, "Wouldn't you enjoy some adult company?" you will most likely get this reply, "No, I get all my emotional needs met by the students."

This man is promiscuous. Let's see why. Before we begin, though, let me point out that high school aged boys and girls need adults in their lives who love them; people with whom they can share their hopes, dreams, disappointments, and failures. With that said, though, they do not need adults around all the time looking to the young people to meet their emotional needs.

There are some things that a thirty-five-year-old can understand about another thirty-five-year-old, that a fifteen-year-old cannot understand. Likewise, there are some things in the life of a forty-year-old that almost any adult will appreciate better than a teenager. It's also important to remember this point: if any one of us looks to those we serve to meet all our emotional needs, we are no longer doing ministry.

BARRIERS TO INTIMACY

Throughout this chapter we have referred, on occasion, to those things that interfere with the possibility of intimacy in our lives. Just above, for example, we suggested that a failure to arrive at mature intimacy usually results in avoidance. There are also a number of barriers that limit a person's ability to enhance the possibility of intimacy in his or her life. Let's take a quick look at a few of them.

A. Thinking Distortions

All of us, from time to time, lose touch with reality. Our thoughts and ideas skew the way in which we experience our world. For example, if I have a poor self-image, I may imagine that others look down on me; in reality, I might be the only person who views myself in this way.

The same is true when we talk about intimacy. In Chapter I, for example, we mentioned that equating intimacy with genitality misses the boat on the rich meaning of sexuality; it's also a thinking distortion that will interfere greatly with our ability to understand the meaning and place of intimacy in life.

B. Fear of Self-disclosure

Without doubt, some of us have more difficulty with self-disclosure than others. A number of young men, for example, don't readily discuss their personal lives with another man; neither do they express to their male friends strong positive emotions like affection and gratitude. There are many reasons for this situation. It's important to remember, though, that self-disclosure is a skill that can be learned and practiced; some people have had less opportunity to practice it than others.

A number of men and women, however, have problems

with self-disclosure because they give credence to this myth: if they tell anyone something important about themselves, that person will have power over them. For example, many people who grew up in an alcoholic family often worry what others would think if they knew what life was like at home. They imagine that any disclosure of this information could lead only to rejection.

Self-disclosure, however, is an essential ingredient in any relationship of intimacy. If I believe that telling you something important about myself will give you power over me, I will experience problems with intimacy.

c. Problems with Dependence

Earlier in this chapter we suggested that many young men and women have difficulty with intimacy. Some researchers would reduce their predicament to this simple notion: men fear dependence; women fear abandonment.

Early in life, most men work to establish their autonomy; independence is very important to them. As a consequence, the vast majority of younger men are threatened by situations in which they must be dependent on others. At times, for example, you will hear a young man say that he moved away from a relationship because he found a woman too clinging; she began, in his mind, to demand too much of him — be it his time, energy, inner world.

A good deal of what we said earlier in this chapter about men and identity formation also plays a role here. In their twenties and thirties, most young men are beset with concerns about who they are and where they are going. They are also just not ready for mature intimacy until they are at home with themselves; as a consequence, for a number of men, midlife and the years following present the best opportunity for this type of intimacy.

Women face a different but related issue: fear of abandonment. Earlier in the chapter, we mentioned that women develop their sense of identity through relationships. A number of younger women will often complain about how inaccessible their male partners are. One twenty-eight-year-old woman put it this way: "I never know what he is thinking!"

In relationships between younger men and women difficulties arise because of the two fears mentioned earlier: of dependence on the part of men, abandonment on the part of women. If a woman moves closer to her partner in a relationship, he might start to complain about feeling "smothered" and say to her, "You want all of my time." This man is frightened to come closer because of his fear of dependence.

As he moves away, however, his female partner is beset with fears of abandonment. She, therefore, may try to move closer; this action will only further alienate her partner and may cause him to flee from the relationship.

As men and women become more secure about their personal identity, so also do their fears about dependence and abandonment respectively begin to subside. This change sets the stage for more rewarding relationships. Unfortunately, for many people, only during midlife are they able to look back on the years just passed and understand more fully the dynamics that interfered with their early adult relationships. At that time, they realize how much of a barrier to intimacy were their fears of dependence and abandonment.

D. A Misuse of Listening Skills

We all appreciate a good listener. Be it at a party or during a meeting at work, most of us are grateful to anyone who takes time not only to listen but also to understand what we are trying to say.

In considering barriers to intimacy, though, we must also ask this question: When does listening become pseudo-intimacy? A counseling relationship, for example, is not an intimate one; it lacks the necessary ingredients of mutual self-disclosure and vulnerability. The ability to listen well, though attractive, is no guarantee that a person has the capacity for intimacy.

E. Homophobia

Though we will address the topic more fully in Chapter III this is an excellent time to note that homophobia is a barrier to mature intimacy. What does the word mean? An irrational fear of homosexuality, and of gay men and lesbian women.

Homophobia, often enough, has more to do with myths, fears, and stereotypes than real people. Consider, for example, members of a religious community who periodically pass remarks or tell jokes about gay people. If they were to discover that one of their number is homosexually-oriented, their behavior might change. As another example: some men and women become hostile and angry about the subject of homosexuality — hostile and angry, that is, until they are told that a son, daughter, parent, or good friend is gay or lesbian. Somehow, the issue of homosexuality takes on a different hue when real people, not myths, fears and stereotypes, are considered.

F. Dysfunctional Background

When we enter religious or seminary life, we bring our family with us. Not physically, of course; nevertheless, they do move in and take up residence at about the same time we do. Our family influences and shapes us; people who fail to acknowledge that fact end up taking many of the attitudes and outlooks learned early in life into every community or rectory in which they live.

It goes without saying that our families help mold our attitudes about human sexuality; they influence our understanding about what it means to be a man or woman, the nature of intimacy, and a life of celibate chastity. While many people blame religious formation for their difficulties in these areas, often enough rectors and novice masters only build upon a foundation already in place.

With that said, it is also important to realize that perfect families don't exist. Some researchers suggest that if one is found, the Smithsonian would be its natural home; such a family would be a rare discovery indeed. Many families, however, do provide their members with what is called "good enough" parenting; while not perfect, the children in them get what they need to move on into adulthood.

Psychologist Kathleen Kelley points out that functional families are marked by several characteristics: honesty characterizes the exchange between members; problems are acknowledged and dealt with; feelings are affirmed — it's OK to have them, it's also OK to express them; communication is clear and straightforward — people do not speak in code! All these factors enhance the possibility of developing relationships of mature intimacy.

What about families that fail to provide this kind of parenting? Stated simply, how do troubled families affect their members' adult relationships? In a number of ways. Before exploring just how, though, it's important to realize that troubled families come in all sizes and shapes. Some, for example, are detached — members survive by avoiding one another; others are enmeshed — normal boundaries between members don't exist. As a consequence, the need people have for privacy is disregarded.

Many factors can give rise to a troubled family: alcoholism and other chemical dependencies; a mother's death when the children are young; parents who value youngsters more for what they achieve than for who they are; physical, emotional, or sexual abuse; a member suffering from depression or a chronic illness. The rules in these families are often unrealistic, inflexible, and inhuman; they encourage self-deception and dishonesty with others and oneself. To illustrate this point, let's take a closer look at families where alcohol is a problem.

The members of alcoholic families are usually guided by four unhealthy rules: denial, silence, rigidity, and isolation. Despite some obvious destructive outcomes, families persist in their use. Let's say a word about each.

1. *Denial*

People use denial to protect themselves from a reality that is too painful to accept. In a catastrophic situation, it can be a healthy defense; it gives people a temporary protective shield until they are able to make sense of the tragedy.

In many alcoholic families, however, denial is life's cornerstone, a foundation for the basic conflicts of many family members: the discrepancy between what they see happening within their family, and what they are told is taking place. For example, in addicted families children are told, "We are one happy family, we enjoy being together." What do they see? Adults belittling and fighting with each other. This rule is cardinal in most of these families: There is nothing wrong here and don't you dare tell anyone!

2. *Silence*

The "don't talk" rule enforces silence and secrecy. Members learn early not to "air their family's dirty laundry"; they are forbidden to discuss troubling situations with each other or people outside the family. The rule of silence also bans talk about feelings and emotions.

Alcoholic families don't talk about the real issues. Members often reach adulthood without ever having discussed with anyone a parent's addiction or the abuse they suffered.

Psychologist Sheila Murphy points out that adult survivors of sexual abuse also have difficulty with the rule of silence. She cites current research estimates suggesting that between 25 and 34 percent of all females and one in seven males are adult survivors; she also points out that the numbers may be higher for women religious.

Silence and secrecy are central components in any pattern of abuse. Like other children from troubled families, incest survivors come to believe that talking will only make things worse. Disclosure of the family's secret will bring rejection. In time, many incest survivors dissociate from the abuse; they enter religious life and make a commitment to a life of celibate chastity with no conscious memory of the trauma they suffered.

How can men and women from dysfunctional families get free of the rule of silence? By recognizing the addiction or abuse in their family, talking about what happened to them, and expressing their feelings. Murphy puts it this way: we may be products of our past but we do not have to be victims of our future.

3. *Rigidity*

Troubled families are often inflexible. They become more and more rigid as they adjust to the problems in their midst. In alcoholic families, members pay a high price: deterioration paralleling that of the addicted man or woman. Faced with the alcoholic person's blaming and self-righteous behavior, they feel shame and hate for themselves. Eventually, family members feel helpless, abused, hurt, rejected, lonely, out of control.

The addicted family's rigid structure stops children from growing up emotionally. In adulthood, the rule of rigidity becomes a need to control. Rigid rules of behavior can control unpredictable situations; they also, however, undermine several characteristics of genuine intimate relationships such as spontaneity, playfulness, and real happiness.

4. Isolation

How do members of alcoholic families survive? By isolating themselves from each other and their community. This pattern leads to adult difficulties with trust and intimate relationships.

While many families leave their members with a positive emotional legacy, others pass on misunderstandings about important areas or enforce rules and rigid roles that are barriers to mature relationships of intimacy. The structure of a troubled family works against developing this type of relationship; members deny feelings and facts about behavior, fail to talk about what is going on, lack trust, and, for survival, isolate themselves from one another and from those outside the group. What do people who grew up in such an environment need to do to recover? Break their family rules; that task is neither quick nor easy. Readers seeking more information about the effects in adulthood of growing up in an addicted family are referred to *Alcoholism's Children: ACoAs in Priesthood and Religious Life,* listed among the references below.

REFLECTION QUESTIONS

1. What barriers to intimacy exist in your life? Write them down; just how do they interfere with your ability to risk closeness with others?
2. a. Spend some time considering life in your family of origin. Who lived at home as you were growing up — write down their names and describe the ways in which they interacted with one another. What

difficulties existed in the family and how were they dealt with?

b. Now consider the emotional legacy your family left you. What aspects of it help foster relationships of intimacy? Which ones interfere?

"SECOND THOUGHTS": SHEILA MURPHY'S STUDY ABOUT INTIMACY AMONG PRIESTS AND MEN AND WOMEN RELIGIOUS

Psychologist Sheila Murphy, mentioned just above, recently published the results of her study about intimacy among priests and men and women religious. While her sample is small and those participating appear serious about their spiritual and emotional growth, her data points to some interesting trends. The vast majority of men and women in the study have much more intimacy in their lives than conventional wisdom would predict; this finding bodes well for their life of celibate chastity.

Murphy based her work on Michael McGill's landmark study of male intimacy. She adopted his definition of intimacy — a level of self-disclosure rather than genital involvement — and used a number of items from his questionnaire in her research. Murphy also developed many new questions using material from the psychology of women.

McGill found that most men in his study did not have best friends. If they did cite one, a woman was usually named. When his respondents identified another man as a best friend, McGill followed up by calling the person and talking with him about the relationship. Most of those with whom he spoke were stunned to have been so identified; more than one reported that he and the man in the study had not been in contact for years.

McGill also pointed out that the majority of the men he studied disclosed regularly to a woman; she was not his spouse but a co-worker, relative, or neighbor. These relationships, however, tended to be one-sided: the man talked and the woman listened. If genital sexuality entered the picture, the man stopped self-disclosing.

Murphy reports that when it comes to intimacy, the vast majority of the priests and brothers she studied failed to comply with either their cultural conditioning or early formation. For example, 89 percent who responded to her questionnaire said they had a best friend and, unlike men in general, 59 percent of those in the study identified another man as their best friend.

Ninety-seven percent of the women religious surveyed by Murphy also named a best friend; like women in general, the vast majority put another woman in this role. More importantly, however, the men and women in Murphy's study report that they enjoy their intimate relationships and believe they know just about everything there is to know about their best friends. Apparently they also share their "talk time" about equally — they listen as well as speak — and work through differences with one another.

Murphy reports a number of other interesting findings. She points out, for example, that in all the elements of intimacy identified by McGill, the brothers, sisters, and priests in her study were more similar to women than men in the general population. She concludes with this thought: many men and women religious and priests fail to live out the scripts of detachment and isolation given to them in early formation. Furthermore, those who participated in her study pointed to a strong spiritual dimension in their relationships: their growth in human intimacy paralleled their deepening experience of God. Sheila Murphy's book, *A Delicate Dance: Sexuality, Celibacy, and Relationships among Catholic Clergy and Religious*, is well worth reading; it adds to and enriches what has been said above about identity and intimacy.

As we push on to the next chapter, let's keep in mind some of the key points of this one. First of all, identity answers the "Who am I?" question; intimacy has more to do with risking closeness than genital sexuality. Next, the three essential elements in any relationship of mature intimacy are: self-disclosure, vulnerability, mutuality. Finally, many barriers interfere with the growth of such relationships: thinking distortions, fear of self-disclosure, problems with dependence, misuse of listening skills, homophobia, and a dysfunctional family background. Now we need to turn our attention, in the next chapter, to some fundamental concepts of sexuality.

REFERENCES

Kelley, Kathleen. *Barriers to Intimacy.* (Unpublished lecture) Bronx, NY: February, 1992.

Mayer, Adele. *Sexual Abuse.* (Holmes Beach, FL: Learning Publications, 1985).

McGill, Michael. *The McGill Report on Male Intimacy.* (New York, NY: Holt, Rinehart and Winston, 1985).

Murphy, Sheila. *A Delicate Dance: Sexuality, Celibacy, and Relationships among Catholic Clergy and Religious.* (New York, NY: Crossroad, 1992).

Rubin, Lillian. *Just Friends: The Role of Friendship in Our Lives.* (New York, NY: Harper and Row, 1985).

Sammon, Sean D. *Alcoholism's Children: ACoAs in Priesthood and Religious Life.* (Staten Island, NY: Alba House, 1989).

Sammon, Sean D. "Understanding the Children of Alcoholic Parents," *Human Development* 8 (1987): 28-35.

Sanford, John. *The Invisible Partners.* (Ramsey, NJ: Paulist, 1980).

Updike, John. *A Month of Sundays.* (New York, NY: Fawcett, 1975).

Whitehead, Evelyn E. and James D. *Christian Life Patterns.* (Garden City, NY: Doubleday, 1979).

Chapter III

SEX AND SANITY

A final story.

It's about a little girl named Emily. She's seven years old and a student at the local parish school; a sex education class is among the many that fill her day.

One day, the teacher introduced some notions about genealogy. She also told the class, "Tonight, for your homework, I want you to go home and find out as much as you can about your ancestors. It's very interesting to know where we came from; this exercise will help you answer that question."

That evening, Emily waited eagerly for her father to return from work. As soon as he entered the house, she ran to him and said, "Daddy, daddy, will you help me with my homework?" He picked her up, kissed her, and said, "Sure I will, Emily, but let's have supper first. Once the dishes are done, I'll give you all the help you need."

After supper, as the last few dishes were being put away, Emily's father said to her, "Come on, Emily, let's sit in the living room and work together on that homework assignment." They both went in and sat down. Emily was perched on the edge of her seat, eager to begin work.

The little girl looked up from her assignment book and asked her father this question, "Daddy, where did I come from?" Emily's father blanched; he said to himself, "Good heavens, I thought I'd have at least a few years grace before I had to answer that question!" So, what did he do? He took "a pass" on the question. "Emily, dear," he said, "that's a good question; its answer is very simple. About seventy-five years ago, a stork came to Pennsylvania and brought your grandfather; three years later, another stork came to Kansas and brought your grandmother."

Since Emily knew only one set of grandparents, he decided he'd skip the other couple. Her father continued, "About thirty-five years ago, a stork came to Illinois and brought your daddy; another stork came to California about thirty-two years ago and brought your mommy. Then just seven years ago, a stork came here to Massachusetts and brought little Emily, the family's pride and joy."

As her father spoke, the little girl frantically wrote down all that he said. When she had finished, she looked at him and said, "Is that it, Daddy?" Emily's father assured her that it was. The little girl put her copybook into her school bag, thanked her father for his help, and, a short while later, went to bed.

She was up early the next morning and left for school at the usual time. As the day moved on, Emily finally arrived in her sex education class. Near the end of the lesson, the teacher said, "OK, boys and girls, please take out your homework assignments so that we can talk about them." With that said, she quickly went around the class asking children here and there what they had learned the night before.

In due time, she called on little Emily. The teacher said, "Emily, what did you learn from this homework assignment?" The little girl stood in the aisle beside her desk and said, "I learned something truly amazing. At least five people have been born into my family during the past three-quarters of a century. No one in the group, though, has engaged in sexual intercourse during the last seventy-five years!"

Little Emily was obviously given some sexual misinformation! This chapter will offer a few facts that are a bit more accurate. To begin with, we will look at factors that enhance and impede healthy psychosexual growth. We'll also discuss sexual awakenings, sexual identity, and define two important terms — genital identity, gender identity. As the chapter closes, we'll talk about the topic of sexual orientation.

One important point as we begin: people called to a life of celibate chastity need accurate and adequate information about human sexuality. This chapter is one step in that direction. Let's start by examining some factors that foster healthy psychosexual growth.

FACTORS THAT ENHANCE HEALTHY PSYCHOSEXUAL GROWTH

Speaking to a group of religious leaders several years ago, psychologist Richard Gilmartin offered these four guidelines for healthy psychosexual growth: be realistic; don't idealize; see the deeper meaning of some sexual behaviors; realize that we all make mistakes. Let's look at each in turn.

A. Be Realistic

Most of us tend to be pretty unrealistic when it comes to human sexuality; we treat the whole area as if it were something apart from the rest of life. To illustrate this point, Gilmartin asks the following question: Suppose the normal biological function of eating behavior suffered the same consequences as human sexuality?

The following scenario would probably result: people covered their hands and mouths when in public because to expose these parts of the body would be considered immodest. Those who chewed sugar-free gum would sin mortally; it has no nutritive value. People with a preference for scotch, rye, or bourbon would transgress only venially; all apparently do have some nutritive value and fit in, consequently, with some notions about natural law.

A person who ordered pornography through the mail would receive cookbooks in plain brown wrappers; Frank Perdue, of course, would be crowned the Hugh Hefner of the 1990's. "A ridiculous description," you say. In some ways, however, it mirrors the attitudes that a number of us have toward human sexuality. For healthy psychosexual growth, this rule is cardinal: be realistic!

B. Don't Idealize

If a fourteen-year-old boy bloodies his friend in a school yard fight, we could say that he had violated the virtue of charity. We would not, however, tell him his life was ruined or carry on as though we could imagine no worse an offense.

What about a person who violates the virtue of chastity: how do we respond? Most of us appear to believe that the virtue of charity might not be so important as the virtue of chastity.

The examples are legion in religious community and rectory living. We can have a priest, sister, or brother who is not even civil to the men and women with whom he or she lives; this behavior is often allowed to continue. At times, we excuse it by citing the human condition or throw up our hands in exasperation because we have little hope of the situation changing.

Just let a member of that same community, however, violate the virtue of chastity. The reaction is often quite different, ranging from shock to an "I told you so" attitude; everyone seems to have some advice and counsel about the situation. Let's take a first step toward a realistic outlook on human sexuality and stop idealizing the virtue of chastity; instead, let's pledge to agree that the virtue of charity is at least as important as the virtue of chastity.

c. See the Deeper Meaning of Some Sexual Behaviors

At times, some people respond to stress by a temporary increase in sexual behavior. For example, a pastoral counselor may see a client who expresses concern about what appears to be a masturbatory habit of increasing frequency. As the counselor begins to explore with the client, however, several things become apparent. The latter is overextended and suffering from high levels of stress; masturbation is a way in which he or she realizes some tension release.

In their sessions together, though, the therapist and client spend relatively little time talking about masturbation. Instead, they examine some of the reasons for the imbalance in the client's life; in time, the troubling masturbatory behavior begins to subside. The behavior appears sexual; to say that it has a sexual meaning, however, misses the point.

In another example, psychologist Patrick Carnes uses the term sexual addiction when referring to this situation: people who feel driven and experience a sense of powerlessness related to their sexual thoughts and actions. Addiction counselor Mic Hunter offers seven characteristics to help people decide whether or not they have a sexual addiction.

1. You take part in sexual behavior(s) despite your will and better judgment.
2. You set strict rules concerning sexual behavior(s) only to repeatedly violate them or fail in your attempts to change your behavior.
3. You have a history of negative consequences related to your sexual behavior.
4. Your behavior appears ritualized.
5. Other than tension reduction, there is a lack of pleasure during or following sex.
6. You are preoccupied with sexual matters or have obsessive thoughts related to sex.

7. You or a therapist can't identify stress that may explain the behavior.

Once again, we have behavior that appears sexual; it may, however, have quite another meaning.

Those who are compulsive about food must learn to eat in a healthier manner; they need support in this process. Overeaters Anonymous can be a great help in that regard. So also, those who are compulsive about sex must learn to behave in ways that are healthier sexually. Hunter reports that our view of sexually compulsive people is changing. We are beginning to understand the deeper meaning of their sexual behavior; with the right kind of help and a Twelve-Step group, like Sex and Love Addicts Anonymous, they can and do recover.

D. Realize That We All Make Mistakes

If we were all to admit that everyone makes mistakes in the area of human sexuality, we'd probably be better able to grow, even flourish, in this important aspect of our life. Unfortunately, though, most of us are victims of a conspiracy of silence that surrounds the topic of sexuality; it prohibits most honest discussion, let alone talk of mistakes.

When people hear the phrase "make mistakes" in regard to human sexuality, many think immediately about some sort of genital transgression. In reality, most of the mistakes we make in this area result from our fear of intimacy: they are relational blunders. Look back, for example, to Chapter II's discussion about foreclosed identity; we pointed out that most people who foreclose also have difficulty with relationships of intimacy. Quite obviously, they make mistakes in the area of sexuality; unsure about who they are, they cannot allow others to come close in a way that might influence them.

One of the most realistic things we can say about human sexuality, then, is that all of us make mistakes in this area.

Married people, single people, priests, and men and women religious — we've all made mistakes when it comes to our human sexuality. Some of us have been afraid to risk our self-understanding in a relationship, and thus avoided an opportunity for intimacy. Others have transgressed genitally. The sooner we admit these facts, the better off we will all be.

FACTORS THAT IMPEDE HEALTHY PSYCHOSEXUAL MATURITY

If some factors enhance healthy psychosexual growth, are there others that impede it? Certainly! Suzanne Breckel, a Sister of Mercy and a psychologist, often pointed to four factors that interfered with psychosexual growth: an attitude of sexual immaturity; the use of a role to define who we are; communicating asexuality; using certain compensatory behaviors in place of a healthy expression of our human sexuality. We'll take each in turn.

A. An Attitude of Sexual Immaturity

In the last chapter, we learned that identity and self-intimacy are crucial to our growth in relationships: most of us won't let others come close to us unless we have a sense of who we are and where we are going. A number of people, however, suffer from an attitude of sexual immaturity; frightened by solitude and unwilling to be alone, they never give themselves an opportunity for greater self-intimacy.

Consider this example. Have you ever lived in a community with a person who cannot be left alone? Some people refer to these individuals as "settlers"; they spend their time sitting in the community room commenting on the comings and goings of everyone else in the group! When left alone, though, these men and women often don't know what to do with themselves;

shrewdly, they insist that others be present to them continually.

We all know that community life, like every other life, includes times when people are by themselves. On these occasions, those who suffer from an inability to be alone are often subject to attacks of anxiety and loneliness. In many ways, they are alienated from their own internal resources.

The Whiteheads define self-intimacy as a virtue by which a person grows in the awareness and acceptance of the particular person he or she is becoming. They also point out just how the process of metanoia and a growing sense of self-intimacy work together.

Most of us have been given this definition of metanoia: a change of heart. The Whiteheads point to another meaning: answering the call to a more tolerant love of the particular amalgam of strengths and weaknesses I find myself to be. Forgiveness plays an important part in this process; a metanoia invites me to confront any blame or guilt I experience as an invitation to absolution. In the Whiteheads' words, forgiveness gives us the power to change the past and the force of its failure.

A willingness to embrace solitude is essential for self-intimacy to flourish. Those who clutter their lives with distractions and run from being alone, miss out on addressing this important task of development.

Self-intimacy has many blessings: aside from helping me be comfortable with being alone, it invites me to reassess my life and understand better just what it is that motivates me to do the things I do. It also gives me the strength I need to overcome loneliness and helps foster healthy psychosexual growth.

B. Use of a Role to Define Who We Are

We discussed roles at some length in Chapter II and so will refer to them only briefly in this section. In the last chapter, we made this significant point: roles are important; it's their overuse that can cause trouble. Remember what we said about people who are teachers, therapists, or students twenty-four hours a day — aside from wearing thin the patience of others, these men and women also manage to keep them at a distance. It's this distance that is an impediment to healthy psychosexual growth; when I use my role to keep others at arm's length from me, I never allow them to come close enough so that I could possibly be influenced by the relationship.

Consider, for example, the priest, community member, or colleague who wears his or her role all the time. Are you ever really sure what it is that he or she is thinking or feeling? How about the person's hopes, dreams, fears? When we live with someone who plays a role around the clock, we begin to feel as though we have taken up residence with an actor rather than a real person.

C. People Who Communicate Asexuality

The dictionary defines asexuality as "having no sex." James Nelson, however, suggests that it's more accurate to think of asexual people as lacking in sensuousness, a characteristic that has more to do with play and pleasure than anything else.

Play is unstructured; when I play, my mind wanders without inhibition and my body is free and loose. Play is also associated closely with the world of the child and the child within us all. To play, I have to trust that my world will not harm me and relax long enough so that I can enjoy my own vulnerability.

When people grow in sensuousness, they increase their ability to play. They also become more comfortable with pleasure: the erotic is diffused throughout their entire body.

Asexual people find it hard to play or experience pleasure; instead, they rely on control and competence in their relationships and, consequently, end up appearing rather wooden. For them, the erotic life remains largely genital in nature. All these factors work against the possibility of intimacy and healthy psychosexual growth.

One final note: if men or women living a life of celibate chastity communicate asexuality, don't blame it on their celibate chastity. Asexuality has little to do with the way people dress or their life choices; rather, it has more to do with their inability to experience pleasure and to play.

D. Compensatory Behaviors for a Healthy Expression of Human Sexuality

Suzanne Breckel points out that many of us use certain behaviors to compensate for a healthy expression of our sexuality. We'll say a word about each in turn.

1. Over dependence on Chemicals as a Substitute for What We Need Affectionally

Some men and women abuse alcohol and other chemicals in an attempt to meet their need for affection. Many alcoholic persons, for example, end up developing a stronger relationship with a bottle than with other men and women; over time, their life becomes centered around drinking and situations that provide an opportunity for it.

People who grew up in alcoholic and other troubled families often use chemicals in an attempt to make up for the affection they need. Some come to misuse alcohol; others run the risk of abusing food or prescription and nonprescription medications. If a person is using any of these items to fill up an ache inside, among a number of other questions, he or she needs to ask: Is this compulsive behavior my way of compensating for a healthy expression of human sexuality?

2. *Over Dependence on Sports, Theater, TV, etc.*

For most of us, sports, the theater, TV, shopping, and hobbies are all wholesome involvements. Many people enjoy playing sports; others relax watching them. Still others relax while shopping or find a renewed sense of energy from a hobby like woodworking, gardening, or painting.

What, then, does an over dependence on sports, the theater, TV, shopping, etc., look like? Think about people who walk, talk, eat, and sleep sports twenty-four hours a day, seven days a week! They appear to have no other interests; conversation about different topics, particularly feelings, is almost impossible.

If my entire life revolves around any one activity — be it sports, the theater, TV, shopping, hobbies, or a hundred and one other examples — I need to ask myself this question: Is this involvement a substitute for what I need affectionally?

3. *Over Intellectualization*

The intellectual life is an important part of anyone's day-to-day existence. Like sports and the other areas mentioned just above, it's essential for a well-balanced life.

What about people who appear to use their intelligence as a substitute for what they need affectionally? One middle-aged brother, for example, looking back on his twenties and early thirties realized that he had used his books and intellectual pursuits to deal with the loneliness he felt. In midlife, he was better able to face his lack of relationships and find other, more appropriate ways, to deal with this situation.

4. *Overwork*

Some people living a life of celibate chastity throw themselves into work in an attempt to meet their need for affection.

They labor morning, noon, and evening — weekends included! If they didn't have much of a personal life in the first place, their overwork will insure that eventually they'll have none at all.

Work is satisfying to many people, particularly if it's work that's enjoyable and gives them a sense of purpose. Overwork, however, just like over intellectualization or over involvement with sports and TV, can impede healthy psychosexual growth. If you can't remember your last full day off, one of the questions you might want to ask yourself is this: Just how and where do I express my human sexuality in a wholesome way?

5. Over Attachment to Pets

Have you ever lived in a rectory or community where some members attended more to the dog than to the adults with whom they were living? The dog's well-being was inquired about at least several times a day; the humans in residence were not afforded so much concern.

As in a family, a dog, cat or other pet in a community can be a welcome addition. In healthy communities, however, people, and not four-legged or flying and crawling creatures, come first!

Be careful, though, in judging others when it comes to their concern about animals. The next time a friend, colleague, fellow priest, or community member pets a dog try to avoid nodding your head knowingly and saying to yourself, and perhaps to him or her as well: "That's a compensatory behavior for a healthy expression of human sexuality if I ever saw one!" When considering over attachment to pets, and all the other examples in this section, it's better to look to myself first before trying to judge the motives of others.

REFLECTION QUESTIONS

As you've done before, take a few minutes to consider the questions below. Answering them should help you apply the material just presented to your own life. A reminder: conversation with others about your response to each question will enrich your reflection.

1. Identify those factors in your life that enhance and/or interfere with your psychosexual growth. Make a list of them. Just how does each one help or hinder your healthy growth in this area?
2. Consider again those factors that interfere with your psychosexual growth. What concrete steps can you take to reduce these obstacles to development?

SEXUAL AWAKENINGS

Dominican Donald Goergen uses the term sexual awakening to refer to very intense sexual feelings accompanied by a genital desire and a feeling of urgency. Often enough, we associate this experience with the onset of puberty; many adolescents, for example, feel as though their genital sexual feelings are out of control.

Some men and women, however, delay their sexual awakening. Due to upbringing or religious training, they fearfully repress the feelings associated with it; consequently, their sexuality doesn't "wake up" until later in life.

Consider this example: a young man discovers in his early thirties that he is homosexually oriented. You might ask, "What took him so long?" As we mentioned earlier, some people in our society suffer with homophobia. As this young man entered puberty, he may have been frightened by his homosexual feelings and the reactions of others toward them; consequently, he pushed them out of his awareness. As he moved into his thirties, however, a relationship, some reading about the topic of homosexuality, or the process of psychotherapy reacquaints him with this lost part of himself.

In another example, some people entered religious life and priesthood at a time in this century when sexuality was not discussed openly and little opportunity existed for cross-gender relationships; as a consequence, many delayed their sexual awakening. Later in life, they began to experience intense genital desires and feelings of urgency. Whether our sexuality wakes up sooner or later, we are all faced with the same challenge: relating this new capacity for genital sexuality to our capacity to love. Until we accomplish this task, we will always experience anxiety and fear about our sexuality.

The process of sexual awakening also carries with it a great lesson; I learn the difference between having sexual feelings and acting on them. Over time I discover that I can control my behavior.

Sexual feelings, unfortunately, are often talked about in a way that would lead us to believe that they are unlike any other feelings we experience. That's simply not true. Consider the emotion of anger for a moment. Some people report getting so angry that they thought they would lose control and hurt or kill someone. The vast majority of them, however, exercised choice about how they expressed their feelings of anger.

Some, for example, distanced themselves from the hostile encounter and provided time for both parties to cool off. Later on, they might have talked with the person with whom they got angry in an attempt to work out their differences.

In another example, many married men and women report being sexually attracted to a number of people in addition to their partner. How do they respond? Most by making choices about their behavior. Married, single, and celibate chaste people need to keep this thought in mind: when it comes to sexuality, we do have choices, we can exercise control over our behavior.

FUNDAMENTAL CONCEPTS OF HUMAN SEXUALITY

Several years ago, the late Michael Peterson, a priest and psychiatrist, addressed a gathering of U.S. bishops. In that presentation, he defined some terms that will be helpful to our discussion about sexual identity: genital identity; gender identity; sex role identity; sex object preference or sexual orientation. Let's take a look at what he had to say.

A. Genital Identity

Before the age of two, a little boy realizes that he has a penis. In time, he discovers that his father and some other family members and peers do also; others do not. Don't be alarmed, we are not talking about a household wherein the members have dispensed with clothing! Little boys and girls, however, are curious. A number, for example, play the game of "doctor." This behavior is usually rather harmless and springs from the child's inquiring mind. Often enough, the real difficulty with young children playing doctor is the overreaction of their parents to this behavior!

Peterson points out that most developmental psychologists suggest there is evidence that boys and girls recognize a difference in genitals as early as the second year of life. Genital identity is based on biology; a person defines himself or herself as male or female because of physiology.

A final point: a person's appreciation of her or his genital identity changes over the course of life. A two-year-old boy's understanding of his penis, for example, is quite different compared to his recognition of its function and role in his masculinity and future when he reaches the age of twenty.

B. Gender Identity

Gender identity is a term used to describe people's feelings about their maleness or femaleness. Evidence suggests that it's ingrained early in childhood and resists attempts to alter it.

Most people find it hard to describe their feelings about being a man or woman. A man, for example, might use stereotypical images in his attempt to convey to others what maleness means for him. Struggling to make himself understood, he uses words such as self-reliant, independent, able to take care of myself and others. In time, however, he might fall back on this observation: "It's the way I feel about myself; somehow words just don't capture the experience."

Many women face the same challenge. Asked to explain what femaleness means to them, they search for expressions that will convey the experience. Eventually, many will say: "Words fall short; they fail to convey what's inside."

Genital identity, then, is based on biology; gender identity is my feeling state about my maleness or femaleness.

C. Sex Role Identity

Sex role identity is determined by whatever the culture will bear during any particular period of history. For example, in the early part of this century, men were most often seen as the "breadwinner" in a family; women worked outside the home much less often than they do today.

Twenty years ago, you would have looked twice if you saw a woman working on a road project in the United States; today, the same scene attracts little if any attention. Dress is also affected by changing sex role behavior. For example, earrings, until recently worn almost exclusively by women, are now worn also by some men. Sex or gender roles can change quickly; what was considered "unthinkable" in one age can, by virtue of culture and changing social roles, become a very different reality.

D. Sexual Orientation

Let's stop for a moment and define heterosexuality. Michael Peterson suggests that most people would find such a task foolish; after all, isn't heterosexuality the norm and aren't the antecedents of heterosexual behaviors obvious and well understood? Not really. Since most of the scientific literature is preoccupied with homosexuality and other sexual behaviors, little is understood about the antecedents of heterosexual behaviors.

The remainder of this chapter, however, will focus on homosexuality. Not only is little uniformly agreed upon data available about its antecedents; a number of myths, fears, and stereotypes have also grown up around the topic. In the next few pages, we'll try to shed some light on the topic of homosexuality and address some of the myths, fears, and stereotypes that surround it.

DEFINITIONS OF HETEROSEXUALITY AND HOMOSEXUALITY

Psychologist James McCary defines heterosexuality as sexual attraction to, or sexual activity with, members of the opposite sex. His definition of homosexuality is just the opposite: sexual attraction to, or sexual activity with members of the same sex. While clear in content, these two definitions do have some problems; if you are trying to make a decision about a person's orientation, where do you focus: on the brain or the genitals?

An example may clarify. A number of people would contend that some, perhaps even many, of the homosexually oriented men and women in the United States are, in fact, heterosexually married.

Anyone who has spent time working in a diocesan marriage tribunal will not be surprised by that observation. The person knows full well that, from time to time, married couples will seek an annulment on these grounds: one of the partners is homosexually oriented.

The first time a chancery official is confronted with this request, particularly if the couple in question have been married for a number of years and have children, he or she may become perplexed and confused and wonder: how did these people have children if one of the partners is homosexually oriented? The same way everyone else does! However, if that same chancery official inquired a bit further, he or she might find that the gay or lesbian partner fantasized homosexually while engaging in heterosexual foreplay and intercourse. One man, for example, reported that his fantasies for arousal and maintaining an erection were almost exclusively involved with men.

In another example, we often get reports of an incarcerated man developing a genital relationship with a cell mate or another man in the prison population. While this relationship continues throughout his period of confinement, when released, he takes up once again his earlier pattern of genital relationships with women. How can we explain this change in behavior? A few questions directed at the parties involved will give us our answer.

Often enough, the person who was imprisoned will tell us that he fantasized heterosexually while engaging in a homosexual genital relationship with his cell mate. Once released, however, he returned to a genital relationship with his partner of choice — a woman. To better understand the above phenomena, let's take a closer look at the area of homosexuality.

ALFRED KINSEY AND SEXUAL ORIENTATION

In the late 1940's, an entomologist by the name of Alfred Kinsey got this bright idea: one of the best ways to get accurate information about people's sexual practices and experiences might be to ask them! That's just what he and his associates did. Their efforts resulted in the publication of two monumental works: *Sexual Behavior in the Human Male* and *Sexual Behavior in the Human Female*.

Kinsey's findings were not universally welcomed. Sheila Murphy tells us that following the 1948 and 1953 publications on male and female sexual behavior, he was hauled before the House Un-American Activities Committee and accused of communist leanings!

What did Kinsey have to say about homosexuality? Based on his findings, he suggested that 60 percent of all boys and 33 percent of girls have engaged in homosexual activity with another person at least once by age fifteen. He also pointed out that 37 percent of the total male and 13 percent of the female population have been involved in homosexual activity to the point of orgasm at some time in their lives.

In reporting his data for men, Kinsey observed:

- 25 percent of those interviewed reported more than incidental homosexual experience or reactions for at least three years between the ages of sixteen and fifty-five years;
- 18 percent reported at least as much homosexual as heterosexual behavior in their histories for at least three years between the ages of sixteen and sixty-six years;
- 10 percent were more or less exclusively homosexual for at least three years between the ages of sixteen and fifty-five years;
- 4 percent reported being exclusively homosexually

oriented for at least three years between the ages of sixteen and fifty-five;

- an additional 4 percent of the males surveyed were exclusively homosexually oriented throughout their lives after the onset of adolescence. Studies with women suggest that between 1 and 3 percent of the female population is exclusively homosexually oriented.

What can we make of these findings? Psychologist John Nash, FMS, points out that sexual activity and affectional needs and expressions exist in innumerable permutations and combinations. The labels of heterosexuality and homosexuality, for example, which appear to say so much, really say very little; instead, they set up a conflict: attraction to one sex appears to rule out any captivation with the other. This oversimplification has given rise to considerable confusion. With these thoughts in mind, let's return and attempt to make some sense of Kinsey's data.

He and his colleagues devised a seven-point scale to categorize the heterosexual-homosexual balance (see chart, opposite page): exclusively heterosexual is at one end; exclusively homosexual at the other. People rated "zero" on the Kinsey scale report that they can't ever remember having a homosexual impulse or feeling or engaging in homosexual behavior.

Those rated "one" report only incidental homosexual contact; while involving same sex fantasy and impulse, the activity may or may not have involved homosexual behavior. People rated "one" who engaged in homosexual activity often report that their behavior was inspired by curiosity, or was forced upon them by other individuals, perhaps when they were asleep or drunk.

"Twos" on the Kinsey scale report more than incidental homosexual experience. Their heterosexual reactions and experiences, however, still surpass their homosexual ones.

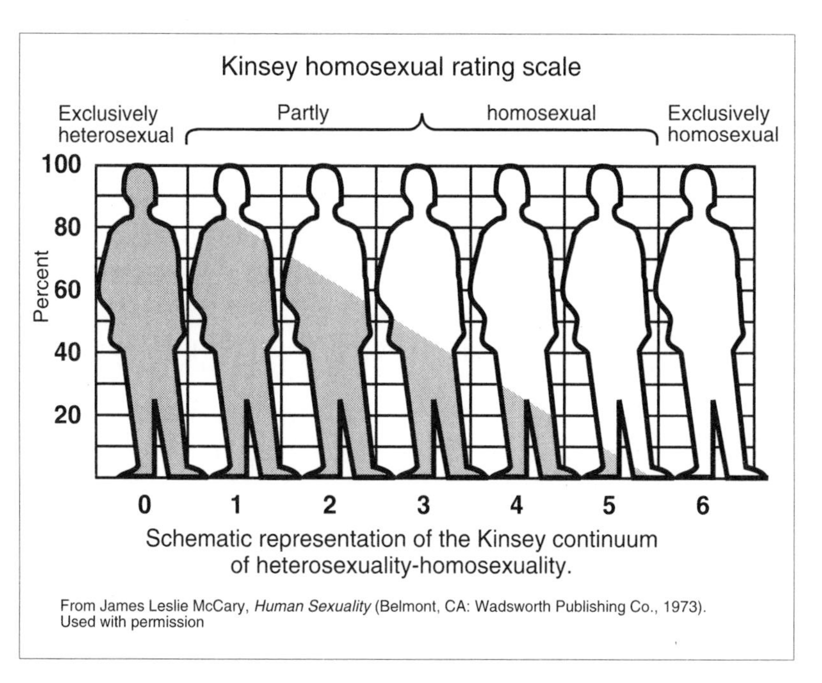

Schematic representation of the Kinsey continuum of heterosexuality-homosexuality.

From James Leslie McCary, *Human Sexuality* (Belmont, CA: Wadsworth Publishing Co., 1973). Used with permission

Kinsey "threes" report about equal hetero-and-homosexual feelings, impulses, and/or behaviors. People are rated "four" if they have more overt activity and/or behavior that is homosexual while still maintaining a fair amount of reaction to heterosexual stimuli.

"Fives" are almost entirely homosexual in their reactions and behaviors; they also experience incidental heterosexual reactions or engage, from time to time, in heterosexual behaviors. Kinsey "sixes" are exclusively homosexual. Even when questioned, these men and women find it impossible to recall from the past or identify in the present any heterosexual impulses, feelings, and/or behaviors.

Using the six-point scale described above, Kinsey and his colleagues suggested that nearly half of American males fell somewhere between the "exclusively heterosexual" and "exclusively homosexual" categories. Women were also found to differ on this scale, although fewer were "exclusively homosexual."

What did Kinsey's work accomplish? Among other things, it reinforced this possibility: our sexual feelings, fantasies, and behaviors are more varied than we might imagine. Now, let's look at what the mental health world has to say about the topic of homosexuality.

SEXUAL ORIENTATION AND THE WORLD OF MENTAL HEALTH

Mental health professionals are skilled at classifying things. When considering behavior they often use the categories of "normal" and "abnormal." Around the turn of this century, a diagnostic manual was developed to help these professionals accomplish their task. This *Diagnostic and Statistical Manual (DSM)* has gone through at least three editions; psychiatrists, social workers, pastoral counselors, and psychologists presently use a revised text of the third edition in coming to diagnostic conclusions.

How does this diagnostic manual work? Consider this example; you are feverish and headachy and have a bad cough. In taking yourself to the doctor, you hope that he or she will examine your symptoms, come to a diagnostic conclusion, and prescribe any necessary treatment.

You will want to be sure the doctor makes an accurate diagnosis; after all, the treatments for a head cold and pneumonia differ significantly! To arrive at an accurate conclusion about what ails you, your doctor will run through a mental list of symptoms; on the basis of that review, he or she will come to a conclusion and make treatment recommendations.

Now, suppose you are feeling weepy and "blue"; you find yourself crying a great deal and wake up early in the morning. You've also lost your appetite and the things that once gave you pleasure no longer do so; some self-destructive thoughts pass through your mind. You probably wouldn't need a psychiatrist to tell you that you might be depressed! If you did consult one, however, he or she would evaluate your symptoms against those listed in the *DSM*. You'd want as accurate a diagnosis from your mental health professional as you'd expect from your physician; if you've got a brain tumor, you don't want to be treated with talking therapy.

In the first edition of the *DSM*, sexual disorders were referred to as perversions. About half-way through the century, a second edition of the manual appeared; this new text used the term deviation when referring to a sexual disorder. Most people are familiar with the standard normal or "bell-shaped" curve. Students who score between 70 and 85 percent on an examination usually fall under the "bell" of the curve; they are the norm. Those who score less than 70 or better than 85 are the deviates. Mental health people used the same notion when they classified sexual disorders in the second edition of the *DSM*.

In the first and second editions of the diagnostic manual, homosexuality was classified as a sexual disorder. When the third edition was released in the late 1970's, however, homosexuality was no longer so listed; instead, "ego dystonic homosexuality" appeared. What is "ego dystonic homosexuality"? It occurs when someone is homosexually oriented and doesn't want to be. Let's take a look at why homosexuality was declassified as a sexual disorder when the third edition of the *DSM* appeared.

Prior to its declassification, at a number of conferences psychiatrists, psychologists, social workers, and other counselors would stand up and say, "I have 100 homosexually oriented men and women in my clinical practice and all of them have a serious emotional problem." In time, however, people began to realize that an equal number of mental health professionals could also stand up and declare, "In my practice, I treat 100 heterosexually oriented people and each of them has a serious emotional problem." We wouldn't judge the state of marriage in the United States by studying the records of people who consult with a marriage counselor. Why, then, take that approach to homosexuality?

EVELYN HOOKER'S RESEARCH

Researchers like Evelyn Hooker believed that we shouldn't be using clinical data to make judgments about the mental health of gay men and lesbian women. Beginning in the late 1950's and continuing for a number of years, she conducted research aimed at throwing some light on this issue.

In one often quoted and significant piece of research, Hooker administered the Rorschach, a psychological test that provides some insight into an individual's personality organization and mental health, to 60 homosexually oriented men who had never darkened the door of a therapist's office; she repeated this process with a population of 60 heterosexually oriented men who also had never consulted a mental health professional.

The tests were scored by a group of judges who were unaware of which test protocols belonged in which group. Their finding? No significant difference in the profiles of the heterosexually and homosexually oriented men involved in the study. On the basis of this result, Hooker concluded that there are emotionally well-adjusted gay men in the population. Her findings and those of others have put to rest the following myth: there are no psychologically "healthy" homosexuals.

Over the past century, a number of theories have been offered in an attempt to explain why it is that some people are gay or lesbian and others heterosexual. There's the psychoanalytic theory, the social learning theory, the genetic theory, and others. Unfortunately, they are just that: theories. No one knows for sure why some men and women are heterosexual and others homosexual. Hooker's findings and those of other researchers encourage us to exercise caution when drawing conclusions about issues of sexual orientation.

HOMOSEXUALITY IN PRIESTHOOD AND RELIGIOUS LIFE

Robert Nugent, a priest and co-founder of New Ways Ministry, reports that a flood of information about homosexuality has appeared since 1969. Its quality varies, ranging from reputable scientific research to propaganda. Nugent suggests that education is one of the greatest needs today when talking about homosexuality in religious life and priesthood, education not only for heterosexually oriented men and women but also for those who are gay and lesbian. Everyone who grew up in this society has been influenced by the myths, fears, and stereotypes that surround homosexuality. Regardless of one's sexual orientation, education is a real need.

Nugent also suggests that misconceptions about homosexuality need to be challenged. For example, some people believe that homosexual orientation equals homosexual behavior. That is simply not true. Where does this myth have its roots? In the misperception, mentioned earlier, that we have little, if any, choice about whether or not to act on our sexual impulses and feelings.

People don't immediately assume that heterosexual orientation equals behavior. Anyone who proposed that idea would be quickly dismissed. Gay men and lesbian women, just like heterosexually oriented men and women, exercise choice when it comes to sexual impulses, feelings, and behaviors. We need, once and for all, to debunk the myth that orientation equals behavior.

Do stereotypes about homosexuality exist? Certainly. Consider this one: effeminacy in a man and an overly masculine look and attitude in a woman are signs of homosexuality. There are effeminate men who are homosexual; many others, however, are heterosexual. The same line of thinking holds true for overly masculine women. Some are lesbian; others are not.

One fear that continues to circulate today, however, is that homosexuality is somehow related to child sexual abuse. A quick read through the Appendix to this book should dispel that notion. Most child abuse in the United States takes place within the home, much of it apparently at the hands of "heterosexually" oriented individuals. Despite that fact, we don't hear people saying that heterosexuality is the cause of child sexual abuse.

We need to stop oversimplifying the area of abuse. As you read through the Appendix, you'll find that there are several different types of abusers: pedophiles, ephebophiles, fixated, regressed, and others. Some abuse is same sex; some abuse is cross-gender. It's an irrational fear, though, to assume that homosexuality is a direct cause of child sexual abuse.

Two final myths about gay men and lesbian women: promiscuity and lack of sexual control. The media portray the lifestyle of many homosexually oriented men and women as licentious and in fact, for some, this is so. There are, however, many other gay men and lesbian women who are anything but promiscuous. For example, an early study, conducted by psychiatrist David McWhirter and psychologist Andrew M. Mattison, documents a number of stable, long-term homosexual relationships. Other gay men and lesbian women have the same kind of "old-fashioned" ethical approach to sexuality that a number of heterosexually oriented people follow.

What about loss of control? Earlier in this chapter, we mentioned that people exercise choice when it comes to sexual feelings and impulses. Spiritual director and counselor, Keith Clark, OFM Cap, gives the following example. When a priest, sister, or brother comes to him with news that he or she has fallen in love, Clark might ask, "How do you want the relationship to develop?" Most of us, faced with that question, would probably reply, "Well, I don't know." Clark would suggest, however, that love is a series of decisions. In saying that, we're not suggesting that relationships are rational exercises; people do, though, make choices regarding sexuality. The decisions we make about our relationships need to be in keeping with our values and life commitments — that's true whether we are single, single again, married, religious or priest.

In another example, ask yourself this question, "What can I do with my sexual energy?" As you answer, you'll probably identify a variety of potential outlets: exercising creativity, genital intercourse, relationships, selfless service, masturbation, appreciating beauty, exercise, etc. Your choice of a channel for this energy, however, has to be informed by your values and life commitments. If any of us believes that we don't have to exercise choice when it comes to the expression of our sexual energy, we are living in a dream world.

Homosexually oriented people exercise choice just as do heterosexually oriented men and women. It would be unfair to judge the entire population of heterosexually oriented men and women on the basis of data collected in a singles bar; let's keep that fact in mind when the myths of promiscuity and lack of control among gay men and lesbian women crop up.

HOMOSEXUALITY AND THE EXPERIENCE OF "COMING OUT"

With all that we've just said about the myths, fears, and stereotypes surrounding homosexuality, still one remaining concern is voiced frequently among many priests and religious: the fear of gay men and lesbian women "coming out." What does that term mean? "Coming out" refers to the process wherein a person comes to know of his or her homosexual orientation and shares that knowledge with others.

Some people "come out" to a few friends, others on the front page of the *New York Times*. A number of people in religious life today fear that homosexually oriented men and women religious and priests who "come out" will cause scandal and that their disclosure will result in a decline of vocations. They suggest that the news that there are gay men and lesbian women in priesthood and religious life will trigger all the myths, fears, and stereotypes mentioned above.

Before we say a bit more about this last matter, let's remember that there have always been homosexually oriented men and women in the Roman Catholic priesthood and religious life — gay men and lesbian women who lived dedicated lives of celibate chastity. Although obvious, it bears repeating that sexual orientation should not be a criteria for admission to religious life and priesthood; the presence of a willingness to live a life of celibate chastity is a healthier yardstick for measuring a candidate's suitability for any congregation or diocese.

Evelyn and James Whitehead offer a model that sheds some helpful light on the current concern about homosexually oriented priests and men and women religious "coming out." First of all, the Whiteheads suggest that, in terms of accurate knowledge about sexual orientation, we are today where we were with our understanding about alcoholism in the early part of this century. In making this analogy, these authors are not implying that sexual orientation is a disease like alcoholism; rather, they are suggesting that our knowledge about sexual orientation is limited at this time in history. The Whiteheads caution: let's not jump to any quick conclusions about issues of sexual orientation based on limited information.

Next, the Whiteheads point out that if no one in religious life or priesthood "comes out" about his or her homosexual orientation, appropriate role models for some young religious will be lacking. The assumption in many communities of sisters, priests, and brothers is that everyone is heterosexual. Consider comments over the dinner table, tasteless jokes about gay men and lesbian women that pass for humor — the message is clear: we're all heterosexual here. Let's face it, we're probably not.

A young gay man or lesbian woman considering religious life or a newly ordained homosexually oriented priest struggling to live out a life of celibate chastity might come to assume that there is no one else like him or her in the community or diocese. If everyone is assumed to be heterosexual, the individual will believe that straight people are able to live a life of celibate chastity; the jury, though, will still be out when it comes to the question of homosexually oriented people's ability to do the same thing. However, if some men or women in the community are public about their homosexuality, this same young person will discover that a dedicated life of celibate chastity is a real possibility for a gay man or lesbian woman. Role models are important; like everyone else, homosexually oriented people need them.

THREE PASSAGES ON THE JOURNEY OF "COMING OUT"

The Whiteheads use the image of a journey or passage when describing the process of "coming out." First of all, they suggest that when it comes to sexual orientation, everyone is called to an interior passage. Whether people are heterosexual or homosexual, it's essential that they grow in the awareness and acceptance of their orientation.

Once people learn something important about themselves, they inevitably want to share it with others whom they value. For example, if I discover I have a knack for writing, the ability to entertain others, or some other talent, I will want to share that finding with people I care about.

A similar situation exists when it comes to sexual orientation. A man or woman who comes to an awareness of his or her orientation wants to share that knowledge with others. Heterosexual people, however, experience little, if any, conflict in this process. After all, our culture and society assume that everyone is heterosexual. For gay men and lesbian women, the path is not always so smooth.

People who are homosexually oriented run the risk of rejection when they share this truth with others. Many can relate stories of friends backing away after learning of another's homosexuality. In spite of the risks involved, the Whiteheads suggest that everyone is also called to this second passage: the passage of intimacy.

Finally, some people are called to a public passage. It might be somewhat public or very public. For example, one gay man may, over time, tells all his co-workers about his homosexuality; another male religious shares it with his family, local religious community, and Province. A lesbian woman might become active politically in support of gay rights legislation and in the process agree to an interview with her local newspaper. During the course of that conversation and in the following day's edition, her questioner and her neighborhood learn of her orientation.

The Whiteheads suggest that in today's often homophobic climate, this third passage is not meant for everyone. To encourage others to make it without also assuring oneself that they have the strength to weather the variety of reactions that will follow is irresponsible. When a man or woman publicly announces his or her homosexual orientation, all the myths, fears, and stereotypes mentioned above will come to the fore.

Consider the religious brother who shares his orientation with the school community where he works. It won't be very long before the principal gets letters and calls from concerned parents expressing fear about this man's teaching and interacting with their son. Some people have the inner fortitude to cope with these reactions; others do not.

With that said, though, it's also important to remember that role models are necessary; people who make a public passage provide them. In religious life and priesthood today, some gay men and lesbian women, living a healthy life of celibate chastity, are called to provide modeling for those who come after them. In deciding to make a public passage, however, people need to go forward with their eyes open; to do otherwise could result in an unforeseen backlash of unfounded myths, fears, and stereotypes on the part of those who receive this news.

CONCLUSION

We began this chapter with the story of little Emily, brought by the stork to Massachusetts just seven years ago! We end it here with our discussion about homosexual passages. "Why so much talk about homosexuality?" you might ask. For this simple reason: to clear up some of the myths, fears, and stereotypes that surround the topic. As mentioned earlier in this chapter, education is today our greatest need when it comes to homosexuality. The information about the subject presented above is offered in that spirit.

As we move on to examine celibate chastity, keep in mind the chapter's key points: some factors enhance and some impede healthy psychosexual growth; sexual awakenings usually occur at puberty — for some, "successful" repression delays this process; genital identity has to do with biology, gender identity with the person's internal feeling state about maleness or femaleness; sexual orientation is not plain and simple — full knowledge about the topic is lacking.

In the next chapter we'll discuss celibate chastity and make this point: the real crisis in celibate chastity today is not sex; it's a crisis of spirituality and significance. On that note, let's move forward.

REFLECTION QUESTIONS

1. What is your emotional reaction to the word homosexual — ease, fear, confusion, recognition? Consider your response for a few moments; what lies behind it? How aware are you of the gay men and lesbian women in your parish, diocese, rectory, or religious community? What is the response of each of these groups to its homosexual members? Can you identify any myths, fears, and/or stereotypes about homosexuality that operate in your religious community, rectory, parish, or diocese? If so, what can be done to correct these misperceptions?
2. What can be done in your local living and/or working situation to foster the psychosexual development of those who live and/or work there?

REFERENCES

Breckel, Suzanne. *Sexuality, the Celibate Response*. (Unpublished lecture, delivered at the National Assembly of Religious Brothers meeting, Providence, RI: June 1977).

Coleman, Gerald D., S.S. *Human Sexuality: An All-Embracing Gift*. (Staten Island, NY: Alba House, 1992).

Conference of Major Superiors of Men. *Men Vowed and Sexual: Conversations about Celibate Chastity*. (Silver Spring, MD: Conference of Major Superiors of Men [video production], 1993).

Goergen, Donald. *The Sexual Celibate*. (New York, NY: Seabury, 1974).

Gilmartin, Richard. *Unpublished lecture*. (Delivered at "When

Church Leaders Care" workshop, Providence, RI, 1984).

Hunter, Mic. *What is Sexual Addiction?* (Hazelden Pamphlet).

McCary, James L. *Human Sexuality* (second edition). (New York, NY: Van Nostrand, 1973).

Nash, John P. *Stress, Ego Identity, and the Disclosure of Homosexual Orientation among Midlife Transition Male Religious in the Roman Catholic Church*. (Unpublished Doctoral Dissertation: Pacific Graduate School of Psychology, 1990).

Nugent, Robert. *Challenge to Love: Gay and Lesbian Catholics in the Church*. (New York, NY: Crossroad, 1983).

Peterson, Michael. "Psychological Aspects of Human Sexual Behaviors," in *Human Sexuality and Personhood: Proceedings of the Workshop for the Hierarchies of the United States and Canada Sponsored by the Pope John Center through a Grant from the Knights of Columbus*. (Chicago, IL: Franciscan Herald Press, 1981).

Whitehead, Evelyn E. and James D. *Seasons of Strength*. (Garden City, NY: Doubleday, 1984).

CHAPTER IV

SEARCHING FOR GOD WITH AN UNDIVIDED HEART

No story to start this chapter; instead, an observation: celibate chastity is in trouble today. A possible reason for its plight? In and of itself, celibacy says very little. We've all known people in religious life and priesthood, for example, who professed lives of celibacy but bore little witness to the Kingdom, lacked availability, and seemed to love no one at all.

Webster defines celibacy as the state of not being married. He also adds these two subordinate definitions: abstention from sexual intercourse; abstention by vow from marriage. People are celibate for a number of reasons: some freely out of generosity and greatness of heart; others just as generously but due to the circumstances of their lives. Some men and women, for example, believe they are called to the single or religious life. Others may judge their life work to be so all consuming as to preclude marriage, family, or a committed relationship to one other person. Still others are widowed, divorced, or were never able to find someone with whom they wanted to spend the rest of their life.

While celibacy, in and of itself, says very little, the lives of individual men and women living a life of celibate chastity can say a great deal. There are today a number of dedicated priests, men and women religious, and lay people who believe they are called to such a life; paradoxically it's as though, in their freedom, they have no other choice about how to live out their life.

In this chapter, we will discuss the topic of celibate chastity with an eye toward better understanding this particular way of being a sexual person. To begin with, we'll take a look at chastity. Everyone is called to it; priests and religious don't have a corner on the market when it comes to this trait.

Next, we'll examine some myths about celibate chastity and marriage. In the last chapter, we talked about myths that surround homosexuality; at least an equal number beset Christian marriage and celibate chastity. As we move on, we'll define celibate chastity and discuss some common approaches to it — as a law, a discipline, a functional value, a gift or gospel value.

A discussion of celibate chastity and spirituality will make up the chapter's core. The real crisis with celibate chastity today is not about sex; rather, it's a crisis of spirituality and meaning. Finally, we'll examine the process of growth into celibate chastity and identify some of the characteristics of those who eventually come home to this way of living.

As we begin, a few points. First of all, as mentioned throughout this book, we need to realize that we grow into celibate chastity. Our understanding and experience of this call must be different at fifty from what they were when we were twenty-five; if not, we need to ask: "Why is this so?"

Second, keep this thought in mind: celibate chastity is violated more truly when the men and women who profess it live lives without significance and fail to root their celibate chastity in the spiritual life than when genital transgressions occur. Many people in the wider society can better understand a genital transgression in the life of a celibate chaste person than they can comprehend that same individual's living a life without significance or spiritual roots. On that note, let's begin.

CHASTITY: A GIFT OF GRACE AND A CHOICE

Theologian Donald Goergen points out that chastity is not virginity. Vast numbers of people in our world are not virgins; that fact does not prevent them from being chaste. Chastity is also not simply celibacy. The former applies to married life as well as to vowed religious and single life.

What, then, is chastity? A number of things. First of all, it's a way of looking at the world and everyone in it. Chaste men and women open their eyes wide enough to see the sacred in every other person they meet.

Next, it's a gift of grace. Gifts are things freely given; we can't earn them and need do nothing to repay the person who offers one. We also have the right to accept or refuse a gift. In the same way, the grace of chastity is a gift — one that helps us integrate our sexual energy into our lives as Christian men and women. As Goergen suggests, chastity helps us utilize our sexuality and put it at the service of our becoming Christian.

Chastity, then, is a gift of grace; God offers it to everyone. Some people accept this gift, others don't. Those who do find that they've received a wonderful agent for integrating their sexuality and spirituality and realizing the goal of both: union with God and others. Chastity is not a foe of sexuality or spirituality; instead, it affirms both dimensions and unifies them. Growth in human sexuality and a developing spirituality go hand in hand.

Chastity is also a choice. Like many choices, this one must be made time and again. People who live chastely do so by repeated actions, day by day, over time. Chastity is not a state I enter but rather a lifelong and daily decision I choose to live out.

To understand this notion better, consider charity for a moment. It's quite evident that charity isn't something we acquire all at once. Only over time, by making hard choices in situation after situation, do we live out the injunction to love our neighbor and ourselves.

Chastity, though, is an attitude as well as a way of behaving. Chaste people need a healthy outlook on their sexuality, an appreciation of their maleness or femaleness, and a wholesome understanding about their bodies and those of others.

A final point: when people are chaste, they see genitality as a sign of God's love by limiting it to faithful and sustained commitments. For Christians, genital activity is a sign of God's relationship with us. Stated simply, human genitality is meant to be a sign of fidelity, God's fidelity to us. By limiting it to faithful and sustained commitments, we give witness to that fact.

MYTHS ABOUT CELIBATE CHASTITY AND MARRIAGE OVER THE COURSE OF LIFE

In Chapter III we discussed several myths that surround the issue of homosexuality. Unfortunately, when talking about celibate chastity and Christian marriage many of us also fail to avoid such pitfalls. Let's take a look at a few of the myths, mentioned by Goergen and others, that surround both life commitments.

A. We Can Try Every Alternative

Early in life, our opportunities appear boundless; knowledge about limits of time, energy, and talent is something that lies well in the future. Consider for a moment, a twenty-three-year-old woman about to enter a career. She thinks to herself, "If this one doesn't work out, there's always time to try something else. I've got a number of years ahead of me."

At midlife the picture changes dramatically. By age forty-five, most of us have learned that *time* is the real currency of life; we are also mindful that we have much less of it than we did at age twenty-three!

A fifty-year-old religious brother, for example, asked to take on a new administrative assignment, knows full well that after he completes his six-year term only a few additional assignments may lie ahead before age and possible ill-health set in. In saying "yes" to this request, he acquiesces knowing that if this new position doesn't work out, he has limited time ahead for trying something new.

The belief that we can try every alternative has its home in early adulthood. With time and energy on our side, many of us are convinced that possibilities are unlimited. The passage of years, however, brings with it this hard learned wisdom: it's just not possible to do it all.

The making of commitments is another factor that challenges the myth that everything is possible. In Chapter II, we suggested that choice and commitment are essential elements in the formation of identity; they also teach us an important lesson about limits.

Whenever I make a choice or commitment, I'm making more than one decision. People who commit themselves in marriage, for example, promise to put their efforts into growing in a love relationship with another person in good times and bad. By deciding to spend their life with one other person, they also elect not to spend their life in the same way with thousands of other people. To believe that time is available in which to try every alternative is a myth that often dies hard during the middle years.

B. Either Choice Brings Perpetual Happiness

Several years ago humorist Erma Bombeck wrote a book entitled *The Grass is Always Greener Over the Septic Tank!* Her title exposes the problem associated with the myth that either marriage or celibate chastity brings perpetual happiness.

When my life is not going well, almost anyone else's life looks better than mine. A middle-aged woman living a life of celibate chastity but experiencing a period of loneliness may come to believe that she would never be lonely if she were married.

So also a middle-aged married woman returning home from work one day to a sullen husband and several feisty children may wonder over the dinner table what her life would have been like had she not married this man and mothered all these children.

Any life choice has its happy moments and its times of disappointment and discouragement. We run the risk of magical thinking if we believe otherwise.

C. The Myth of Normality

In the last chapter, we pointed out that a number of mental health professionals like to classify behavior as normal or abnormal. It's important, however, to ask this question: just what do we mean by normal?

Earlier in this book, we mentioned that a standard normal or "bell-shaped" curve defines the norm statistically; everyone who falls into the area under the center of the bell-shape is classified as "normal." On a history exam, for example, students who score between 70 and 85 percent are the norm; those who fall below 70 or above 85 are exceptional or statistically deviate. In saying that those who lie outside the curve are not "normal," however, we in no way mean to imply that they are pathological.

Far less than 50 percent of the men and women in the United States live lives of celibate chastity; those who do, therefore, are statistically "deviate" or beyond the norm. Today, some people suggest that Christian marriage, with its assumption of monogamy, is also abnormal. If we are to believe many of the media reports about fidelity and marriage, we might well agree that the notion of Christian marriage is deviate; still, we hope neither it nor celibate chastity is pathological. When discussing celibate chastity, or Christian marriage for that matter, we need to diffuse the myths about what is normal and what is not.

D. Our Decision for Celibate Chastity or Marriage is Free

Our life decisions are motivated by a number of factors. In Chapter II, for example, we suggested that some people, fearful of their sexuality, rush into marriage or a life of celibate chastity.

Early in life we often offer only the most idealistic of reasons for our choices. Later in life we can be a bit more honest: all of us make our life choices out of mixed motives. Some are sterling; others are a bit more tarnished.

If, early in life, I entered religious life, or chose a life of celibate chastity or marriage and my decision was not completely free, does that make my choice invalid? Not at all.

Yale psychologist Daniel Levinson points out that most people make major choices about their life before they have enough information to come to the best possible decision. However, if they wait until all the data is in, they'll be dead before they do anything!

As we grow older and learn more about our motives, we need to rework our life commitments. I may, for example, have entered religious life or married for several very good reasons; often enough, it's another set entirely that causes me to stay with my earlier commitment.

E. The Main Problems in the Celibate Chaste Life Can Be Handled Spiritually

This myth spells out clearly the "pray it away" solution to problems in a life of celibate chastity. As we've stated already, spirituality is at the core of genuine celibate chaste living; prayer and a growing relationship with God are essential elements.

Many problems in a life of celibate chastity, however, can't be prayed away; rather, they must be talked about with others as well as God. Consider a young brother who falls in love. He needs, first of all, to talk with his trusted advisors and friends about his feelings and the meaning and place of this relationship in his life. A regular life of prayer is essential to the celibate chaste life; so also, is honest conversation.

F. One Chooses Celibate Chastity Because He or She Couldn't Make It Elsewhere

This myth is based on the following false observation about people who choose lives of celibate chastity: "The poor things, what else could they have done with their lives!" Men and women who are living vibrant lives of celibate chastity are very attractive people. As we mentioned in Chapters II and III, their life includes relationships of intimacy, a growing relationship with God, and the quality of self-intimacy. Their life, like that of others, has its rewards and drawbacks. However, they usually did not choose their life by default.

FOUR ELEMENTS IN CELIBATE CHASTITY

When speaking about Institutes of consecrated life, the new *Code of Canon Law* has this to say about the topic of celibate chastity: "The evangelical counsel of chastity assumed for the sake of the kingdom of heaven, as a sign of the future world, and a source of more abundant fruitfulness in an undivided heart, entails the obligation of perfect continence in celibacy."

When the Code addresses the obligations and rights of clerics, it defines celibate chastity in this manner: "Clerics are obliged to observe perfect and perpetual continence for the sake of the kingdom of heaven and therefore are obliged to observe celibacy, which is a special gift of God, by which sacred ministers can adhere more easily to Christ with an undivided heart and can more freely dedicate themselves to the service of God and humankind."

Earlier than the recent Code, Suzanne Breckel identified four elements in most definitions of celibate chastity: one, it has to do with pursuing and developing ways of loving that are non-genital; two, it needs to be rooted in the spiritual life; three, it needs to be connected vitally to one's call in life and one's call to ministry; four, it has to do with a style of life wherein one chooses not to be coupled. Let's look at each in turn.

A. Pursuing and Developing Ways of Loving that are Non-genital

When most of us learn that someone is living a life of celibate chastity, we assume that that person's ways of loving are non-genital. We'd be perplexed by a man or woman who professed to live a life of celibate chastity while, at the same time, maintaining an active genital life. Some of those professing to live a life of celibate chastity may, at times, violate their commitment; however, for them to insist that genital abstinence is not commonly understood to be part of their pledge is nonsense.

On reading this definition some people might comment: all this preoccupation with genital sexuality! In recent years, a number of men and women have suggested that if more attention were placed on "pursuing and developing ways of loving" and less on genital sex, we'd have a more balanced approach to celibate chastity.

We need to realize that a celibate chaste person's focus has to be on developing and pursuing ways of loving, not just genital behavior or the lack of it. To live a loveless life of celibate chastity is a contradiction in terms, as much as insisting that genital sex and celibate chastity are compatible.

B. Rooted in the Spiritual Life

A person's celibate chastity must be rooted deeply in the spiritual life. If faith and one's relationship with God are not at the center of a life of celibate chastity, it makes little sense. Later in this chapter, we'll develop this notion more fully.

C. Connected Vitally to One's Call in Life and One's Call to Ministry

People's choice for celibate chastity must conform to their call in life and their call to ministry. Stated another way, a "goodness of fit" must exist between celibate chastity and the lives of those who live it.

Consider for a moment the reassuring feeling that comes over people when they realize they have married the right mate. Celibate chaste men and women have a similar experience. Many cannot imagine living another kind of life; instead, they realize that a life of celibate chastity is, for them, the best way to grow. To do otherwise would be experienced as living someone else's life.

Genuine celibate chastity, however, also calls those living it to intimacy. A person professing to live a life of celibate chastity, but lacking in loving relationships, must look beyond his or her celibate chastity for the cause of this deficit.

Selflessness and service, essential ingredients for Christian ministry, are two other important elements in a life of celibate chastity. As with chastity itself, however, only prayer and hard choices made over time in situation after situation help people to acquire these traits.

Selfishness and self-involvement are incompatible with a life of celibate chastity. For example, people who choose this way of living so as not to be bothered by others never seem to be at home with their choice. As true of any life of love, God's gift of celibate chastity has more to do with self-transcendence than self-fulfillment.

D. Choose Not to be Coupled

Celibate chastity has to do with a style of life wherein people choose not to be coupled. For many men and women today, this aspect of celibate chastity is more challenging than in the past.

Our society reinforces coupling. If you have doubts about that statement, just talk to young men and women recently engaged. From that time forward, a number of people see them less as individuals and more as a couple. For example, if they do not attend social functions together over a period of time, others may wonder if their relationship is in trouble.

It doesn't take very long for a celibate chaste person to understand that he or she is not coupled. Psychotherapist and researcher A.W. Richard Sipe points out that early in a life of celibate chastity, those choosing this way of living realize that they are not like most other people: many of their peers are getting married, they are not.

At midlife a different but related challenge presents itself. During their middle years, many people are often more concerned with companionship than genital sexuality. For example, a number of men report that while passion marked the early stages of their sexual life, the need for a mate distinguished its later years.

At age forty or fifty, priests, men and women religious, and single and single again people face the same challenging question as their married counterparts: who are my real companions? In their attempts to answer this question, however, a number of religious and priests have grown reluctant to consider any ministry move that would threaten the local support system they have built with so much care.

Consider, for example, a congregation of teaching brothers with works throughout the United States. If a provincial asks a member of the province to move from New York to Arizona, he's asking for much more than a job change.

Many priests, sisters, and brothers, reminded that married people of a similar age are often forced to move from one part of the country to another because of circumstance or job related needs, point out that their married people do take with them this important support system — a spouse and family.

While it's possible to maintain relationships over distance, some priests and men and women religious fear the loss of friends and familiar circumstances. They are also anxious about starting over again in a new place with unfamiliar people. Some may point out wistfully that it was "easier" when their rule of life discouraged getting close to others. Such a belief is wishful thinking; people in Church ministry today must face this challenging task of maintaining relationships while also being open to change and the demands of mission. In the process this fact will hit home time and again: to live a life of celibate chastity is to choose not to be coupled.

FOUR COMMON APPROACHES TO CELIBATE CHASTITY

Even though we are discussing celibate chastity as a gift, many people experience it as anything but! At times, even those called to this way of living perceive it as the law, a discipline, and a functional value. On other occasions, of course, they experience their celibate chastity as a gift or gospel value. Let's take a closer look at each of these approaches.

A. LAW

A law is something that regulates behavior, like traffic laws and income tax laws. People might not always like a law or might even ignore it; however, it does limit their actions on most occasions.

In our Church today, there are men in ordained ministry who experience their celibate chastity only as the law. If they could, they would choose otherwise. Ordained ministry, however, at this point in time, requires celibacy; if I feel called to formal priesthood but not to celibate chastity, I will experience the latter as a law. Those in this dilemma find it confusing when others speak about celibate chastity as a gift. One young priest, commenting on his predicament, put it this way: "You can pray and pray, but you will never pray a law into a charism!"

Those genuinely called to a life of celibate chastity, however, also experience their choice as the law from time to time. For example, when faced with sexual difficulties and an emotional life in turmoil, their behavior may be regulated more by the legal requirements of their commitment than any larger charismatic understanding of their vow or promise.

B. Discipline

Some people view their celibate chastity as a discipline. There was, for example, a time in formation for priesthood and religious life when those in training were led to believe that they would be "storm troopers for Christ"! To measure up to this ideal, sacrifice would be required; celibate chastity was one of the renunciations. This discipline, along with others, would make them worthy enough to serve the Lord in religious life or priesthood.

Our Church has a long history of disciplinary practices. For example, even though regulations have changed over time, fast and abstinence are still common disciplines among all Christians. There are also monasteries today where the monks continually abstain from eating meat as a form of discipline.

Discipline is, as we'll see later, necessary for any life lived well. Genuine discipline, however, always leads to the integration and wholeness of the person. Fasting, for example, must be a means to an end and not an end in itself. The same principle holds true for celibate chastity.

C. Functional Value

Many men and women value their life of celibate chastity because of its functionality. It allows them to take risks they could not were they married or responsible for a family. The ministry of some others is time consuming and requires frequent moves; it could not sustain marriage and family.

In the history of our Church, there are numerous examples of the functional value of celibate chastity. Many founders of religious orders were single-minded; their celibate chastity freed them to carry out the work to which they were called. Today, many missionaries, particularly those in troubled spots around the globe, value the functional aspect of their celibate chastity. For those closer to home, it can allow them more time for the ministry, prayer, and reflection that must be at the heart of genuine celibate chaste living.

What is the end of the functional aspect of celibate chastity? Availability. Anyone choosing a life of celibate chastity for personal comfort may be celibate but is missing the mark on celibate chastity.

D. A Gift or Gospel Value

Some men and women, over time, develop this awareness: they have been called to a life of celibate chastity and for them it's the best way to grow. Without doubt, their call is intertwined irrevocably with their salvation history.

When people believe that celibate chastity is part of God's dream for them, it becomes for them a gospel value. They have no need to explain or defend their choice; it could not have been otherwise. Looking back near the end of life, they realize that they could not have lived another life and grown to be the same person.

By way of analogy, consider married men and women. They have no need to explain or justify their choice of a mate. Most of them also know that their husband or wife is part of their religious history; to have lived another life with some other person would be similar to living someone else's life.

We all come to God in a variety of ways. Sometimes through our loving relationships with others we realize God's love for each of us. At other times, however, we approach God in an undivided way. The life commitments people make give witness to the myriad ways in which men and women come to God. People in committed relationships like marriage, for example, learn gradually and give witness to the fact that one way to a loving relationship with God is through a single-hearted loving relationship with another person. Men and women called to a life of celibate chastity follow a different path: they witness with an undivided heart to the human search for God.

Whatever our choice of life commitment, we need the witness of people who have made different commitments to remind us of the many ways in which we can come to God. One journey is no better than any other; they are, however, different. It's that difference that's so important. If I am living a life of celibate chastity, men and women in committed relationships bear witness to the importance of loving relationships in my life with God. So also, people vibrantly living out their celibate chastity witness to their married counterparts the need for an undivided approach to God in everyone's life.

REFLECTION QUESTIONS

As in previous chapters, take some time now to consider the questions below. Jot a few notes to yourself about your response to each one; give some thought also to sharing your answers with a trusted friend, some colleagues or community members, a spiritual director or counselor.

1. Which of the three elements of celibate chastity mentioned in detail above speaks to you: developing and pursuing ways of loving that are non-genital; connected vitally to one's call in life and one's call to ministry; choosing not to be coupled? Just how does this aspect show itself in your life today? What are your feelings about this element of celibate chastity? What are its rewards and drawbacks?
2. Some priests and men and women religious report that celibate chastity can be experienced as the law, a discipline, a functional value, and a gift or gospel value. Which description comes to the fore most often for you? In what ways?

CELIBATE CHASTITY AND SPIRITUALITY

What's at the heart of genuine celibate chaste living? Something quite simple: the spiritual life. To be at home with their choice, sisters, priests, brothers, and any lay Christians called to a life of celibate chastity must face what it means to be a spiritual person. If they learn all there is to know about human sexuality but fail to take on the identity of a spiritual person, these men and women will always be ill at ease with their celibate chastity.

What does it mean to be a spiritual person? A number of things. First of all, recognizing the spiritual awakenings that take place during the course of life. In Chapter III we discussed sexual awakenings, those times in life when our sexuality wakes up and comes alive with full force. Spiritual awakenings are similar: intense spiritual desire emerges, gradually or dramatically, as in a conversion experience.

Not everyone welcomes a sexual awakening. Many people are also uncomfortable with their spiritual awakenings, which cause them fear and anxiety. When this is the case, repression can follow quickly.

Everyone's spiritual life has a long history: it begins in childhood, passes through the adolescent and early adult years, and often comes to maturity in midlife and the later years. At whatever time in life a spiritual awakening comes, however, all of us are faced with this challenge: integrating this new capacity for God into our self-understanding. If we fail to carry out that task, we run the risk of spiritual stagnation.

Second, a spiritual person accepts the fact that God loves each man and woman in a unique and special way. Consequently, everyone's spirituality is singular. Earlier in this book, we suggested that there is no one way to be a sexual person; so also, there are many ways to be a spiritual person. Throughout life many of us are presented with formulas and plans of action that carry with them some guarantee of success in the spiritual life; rather than enhancing our relationship with God, though, many just get in its way.

In one breath we might have been told that our spiritual life is unique; in the next, we were led to believe that Franciscan, Dominican, Ignatian, Marial, or one of a thousand other spiritualities was the only genuine way to be a spiritual person. Don't believe it; there are as many ways to be a spiritual person as there are people. Various spiritualities are only aids; they should not get in the way of our unique relationship with God.

Third, spiritual people know they don't have to do anything to earn God's love. It is given freely. God's love is extravagant: it brought us into being, it sustains us in life, it will bring us home. We can accept or reject God's love, but we don't have to do anything to earn it.

Many images are used to describe God — God as parent is a popular one. There are good reasons for using the words mother and father to portray God. Most parents love their children unconditionally; throughout life, they want what's best for them. Even when adult sons and daughters get into trouble or cause disappointment, the majority of parents stand by them.

While most children don't have to do anything to earn their parent's love, some others feel as though they must act in certain ways or hold particular beliefs to merit such love. Whatever our situation, we need to remember that God's love is always unconditional, faithful, freely given.

Earlier in this chapter, we suggested that chastity is a gift. We also pointed out that gifts are generously dispensed; the benefactor expects nothing in return. God's love is like that: a gift given freely with no strings attached. When any of us can accept that fact, we have much less anxiety about our progress in prayer or any other area of our life. We can accept or reject God's love, but having to earn it is just out of the question.

Finally, being a spiritual person includes coming to let God love us on God's terms, not ours. Jesuit Thomas Green wrote a book several years ago entitled *When the Well Runs Dry*. In it, he talked about the life of prayer; he also suggested that God's way of loving us may be different from human love. If we mistakenly insist that God love us in a human way, we may miss the extraordinary relationship into which God invites each of us.

Let's stretch the image in Green's title to make our point. The water in the well is God's consoling grace. Early in the spiritual life, we are young, energetic, strong — the well also brims with water. It's relatively easy for us to take a bucket and satisfy our spiritual thirst with the cool refreshing water of God's grace.

As we grow older in the spiritual life, however, the water level drops and our earlier strength diminishes; it's harder to get water from the well. With human effort we can still satisfy ourselves with the water of God's grace; that task, though, is not so easy as it was years earlier.

The day will come, however, when we have grown to maturity in the spiritual life — we will have prayed long and hard — and the well will have run dry. What can we do then to share in God's comforting grace? Nothing. About all that we are able to do is to sit and wait for the rain. When any of us reaches this point in the spiritual life, we are ready to allow God to love us as God chooses to love us.

How do most of us respond to this situation? By declaring that we are barren, empty, and living in a wilderness! What a remarkable conclusion; just when God has cleared away the distractions and led us into the desert to speak to our heart, we insist that God has abandoned us.

At midlife, all of us face this faith issue: the experience of social and individual sin. Many midlife men and women, for example, report a growing sense of their need to be redeemed. Totally reliant on God, they are invited to new forms of prayer. For some, it's one that is deeper and free of thoughts and images. What must they do to enter into this new form of prayer?

Surrender! Several signs indicate that such an invitation is being extended. Some people find that they can no longer actively meditate. For others, prayer is uneventful and arid: consolation is lacking and old forms of prayer are found wanting. Many people describe their experience in these words: "I long for a simple presence before God; I want to be with God, not think about God."

Teresa of Avila apparently faced the same dilemma as many modern day midlife men and women. Her solution was simple. She often said that when she was unable to find words for her prayer, she would go into the chapel and sit before the Blessed Sacrament so the Lord could look on her with love.

Celibate chastity, then, must be rooted in the spiritual life. If a loving relationship with God is not at its heart, celibate chastity becomes little more than celibacy — the state of being unmarried — and gives trivial witness. Eventually most people wonder just what the lives of those living it are all about.

Stop for a moment and consider what has just been said above about the attributes of a spiritual person. Do you find yourself asking: Doesn't everyone need to become a spiritual person? Absolutely. Mature celibate chaste living requires pretty much the same things necessary for any life lived well. Let's keep that fact in mind as we consider our next topic.

WHAT IS NEEDED FOR A LIFE OF CELIBATE CHASTITY?

Don Goergen points to two necessary elements in any well-lived life of celibate chastity. Let's examine each of them and a few others in turn.

A. Discipline

Earlier we mentioned that any life lived well requires discipline. Consider an athlete or dancer. Each must put in many hours of disciplined practice to excel. A runner, for example, will need to follow a particular diet and persevere in a rigorous training schedule; a dancer must practice the steps over and over again until the routine is just so.

Teachers face the same challenge. To develop adequate knowledge of a subject area and communicate it well, educators have to spend hours reading and learning the material to be taught. They will then need to consider a variety of ways to present the subject matter: lecture, discussion, audio/visual materials. Year after year, competent teachers are reworking their material and developing new and more effective ways to communicate it.

A similar discipline is needed for a life of celibate chastity lived well. Those who wish to grow in this way of being a sexual person must develop the disciplines of a regular life of prayer, time for fellow community members and friends, a meaningful and useful ministry, study — all the ingredients for a balanced life. That much should be obvious; after all, isn't the goal of genuine discipline the person's integration and wholeness?

B. SOLITUDE

Solitude is necessary for genuine celibate chaste living. In Chapter III, we talked about its importance for healthy psycho-sexual growth — solitude is an essential ingredient of self-intimacy.

Solitude helps us face being alone; it resists the tyranny of diversion so prevalent in our society today. Solitude, however, can also be a terrible trial: it forces us to face ourselves. Some people, for example, having ventured out on their first ten-day directed retreat, vow to bring a radio or something to read on the next one. With only the Word of God and a brief session with their Director as daily companions, they found their solitude too threatening. Goergen puts it well: solitary people refuse to live by being amused. Their reward, however is great: the gift of self-intimacy.

A caution here. If solitude does not lead to love and mature intimacy, it is not true solitude. Earlier in this book, for example, we pointed to the importance of self-knowledge for relationships of intimacy. Persons lacking self-intimacy will be unwilling to risk closeness with others. Goergen points out that the social goal of solitude is compassion. Its spiritual goal is contemplation.

c. A Sense of Humor

A sense of humor helps most people to get through some of life's rough spots. It does much the same for celibate chaste people by helping them keep perspective. Celibate chastity is meant to make those living it happy. That's right: happy! Not in the sense of hilarious laughter, but rather that deep feeling of contentment experienced by men and women who have meaning and purpose in their life and good companions with whom to share themselves.

During the past two decades, some men and women religious and priests have appeared to be anything but happy. Consider for a moment some recent continuing education topics offered to priests, sisters, and brothers: stress and burn-out, loss and life transitions, the life and death of religious orders, coping with difficult people, and problems in community life. A healthy sense of humor helps men and women religious and priests maintain their equilibrium; it also contributes to the happiness that should have a prominent place in their life.

Throughout this book, we have also pointed to several other important elements in a vibrant life of celibate chastity: relationships of mature intimacy, a meaningful ministry, and, most essential, an ever deepening spiritual life. Brothers, sisters, priests, and others called to this way of living must work hard to balance these necessary ingredients in any well-lived life of celibate chastity.

As we move toward the end of this chapter, let's turn our attention to the work of A.W. Richard Sipe. His insights about celibate chaste living will be helpful to some readers.

STAGES OF GROWTH IN CELIBATE CHASTITY

Since the mid 1960's, A.W. Richard Sipe, a psychotherapist affiliated with Johns Hopkins University, has studied patterns of growth into celibate chastity among a group of 1000 priests, half of whom were in some form of psychotherapy. When he published his results in *The Secret World: Sexuality and the Search for Celibacy*, Sipe was quick to point out that his work was more of a search than scientific research. While this distinction may appear minor to some readers, in fact, it's quite significant. Sipe identified patterns and trends among many of the men he studied; at some point, however, they will need further study.

Sipe's findings about the process of growth into celibate chastity are helpful to our discussion. To begin with, he points out that people who undertake a life of celibate chastity enter into a process of growth — over time their early external ideal must become an internal reality. Second, Sipe reports that men in his study who had *achieved* a life of celibate chastity lived with integrity — they were who they said they were.

One drawback to this work: it was conducted with a small group of men who were priests. As a consequence, we must be careful not to generalize his findings to all priests, or to sisters, brothers, and other single people. With these thoughts in mind, let's take a look at his stages.

A. Gain/Loss

Sipe calls the first phase of growth into celibate chastity the "gain/loss" stage. When people personally decide to live celibately and chastely, be it at a young age or later, they experience a sense of loss. Some men in his study put it quite simply: they experienced the loss of a genital life. This awareness carries with it a potential depressive quality. That's to be expected: whenever people lose an important person or part of themselves, they often feel sad and disheartened.

B. Like Me/Not Like Me

The second stage of growth into celibate chastity is called the "like me/not like me" stage. It usually occurs within two to five years after ordination or religious vows. During formation, many of the priests in Sipe's study lived in a rather narrow world. Priests, sisters, and brothers currently in midlife or older can remember the restrictions of novitiate or seminary days. They spent their time with other young people who had set their sights in a similar direction. People tend to question their choice for celibate chastity less when they have few in their world who are choosing otherwise.

Shortly after ordination or final vows, however, young priests often begin to work in settings with many other people, a number of whom are choosing a sexual life other than celibate chastity. More to the point, Sipe notes that through their ministry, many young priests come to learn what the lives of other people are all about. One young man responded to this discovery by saying: "Everyone has a sex life except me." Another had this reaction: "I'm not sure I want to spend my whole life sleeping alone." Very quickly, then, many young celibate chaste men discover that some people are like them, others are not.

What challenges do they face? First, to begin the process of internalizing the ideals of celibate chastity; second, to start to develop their identity as a celibate chaste person. Close identification with a celibate chaste community is one of the best ways to accomplish the second task.

Sipe points out that sexual experimentation was not uncommon at this time in the sample of men he studied. For some it involved a few incidents; for others it began a prolonged period of sexual activity that precluded any genuine life of celibate chastity; the experimentation of still others led them out of the priesthood and into a relationship that included a genital life.

c. In Control/Controlled By

This stage gets underway somewhere between thirteen and sixteen years after ordination or vows. It entails a movement from being controlled by external authority to a greater internalization of personal values and beliefs. Authority issues definitely mark this period.

Sipe points out that the men in his study faced this challenge during the "in control/controlled by" stage: becoming their own person. In the face of stagnation, loss, and failure, these men were called upon to surrender their illusions and make their own certain values, beliefs, and goals.

Many men reported a greater reliance on their spiritual life during this stage. So also, they relied more on their communities, but at the same time grew to be less dependent upon them. Sipe points to the priests in Edwin O'Connor's *The Edge of Sadness* and the accounts of J.F. Powers and Georges Bernanos as typical of this period.

He also suggests that Ignatius's requirement that his followers take a year of reflection and rededication after twelve or thirteen years in training reflects the saint's intuitive awareness of the needs of celibate chaste men in this stage.

How do those who grow through this stage emerge? With a new level of relationship with themselves, their God, and their community.

D. Alone/Lonely

Coming somewhere between twenty-two and twenty-seven years after ordination or vows, the "alone/lonely" stage bears witness to everyone's lifelong struggle to move from loneliness to aloneness. Among other things, a life of celibate chastity gives witness to this fact: we are all alone. Whether married, single, or single again, a priest, brother, or sister — we enter this world alone; we also leave it as a solitary person.

Aloneness, however, cannot be equated with loneliness. The first term describes the ability of people to accept themselves and their destiny; the second refers to a situation wherein men and women are alienated from their own resources. To move from the second to the first, people must surrender the illusion that merging with another is possible and accept the fact that aloneness exists in the life of everyone.

What question marks this stage? "Has it been and does it continue to be worth it?" A growing relationship with God is necessary for any satisfactory response.

E. Integration

Without doubt, Sipe found a mystic quality in the life of the men who had arrived at this stage of celibate chaste growth. They were very aware of the transcendent and reported moments that could be classified as ecstatic or peak spiritual experiences.

More important, however, was the way in which the transcendent was obvious in their everyday life: they had a spiritual transparency — they were what they appeared to be. While not without faults and failings, they had become what they set out to be: men of God.

Sipe pointed out that it was easier for him to find priests willing to talk about their sexual struggles than to uncover those who could explain the experience of achievement and integration. We need more direct witness from the latter group: too much of our talk about this topic is idealistic or legalistic; not enough comes from the hearts of those who are well along on the journey.

TEN ELEMENTS THAT SUPPORT CELIBATE CHASTE ACHIEVEMENT

Sipe found ten elements present in the lives of the men he classified as having achieved a celibate chaste way of living. The first, *work*, bore witness to this fact: those who had achieved celibate chastity used their energy and time productively.

Prayer or *interiority*, the second element, is striking: all of the men who achieved celibate chaste living spent at least one and a half to two hours a day in prayer. Time spent in prayer was a priority for these priests.

All who had achieved celibate chastity sensed themselves as part of a *community*; intimate relationships with a wide variety of people appeared to support celibate chaste achievement. *Service to others* was an important part of each man's life and another indication of his self-transcendence.

Not all of the priests in Sipe's study were ascetic. Some enjoyed good food and fine wine. All did, however, attend to their *physical needs*. Sipe points out that these were men who knew themselves and their limits and needs; they also dealt with them appropriately.

A sense of *balance* was apparent in the life of each of these men, a balance that provided sufficient time for prayer and limited any tendency to overwork. Many of the men in Sipe's study also spoke about their security with themselves and the transcendent. These were *secure* men in the best sense of that word: they were consistently themselves regardless of the circumstances.

Each man had a sense of *order* in his daily and seasonal life; while not all scholars, the men who had achieved celibate chastity possessed *a love of learning*. Finally, all the achievers took pleasure in some form of *beauty*, be it music, art, drama, or nature.

CONCLUSION

Sipe's picture of this last group of men in his study is an attractive one, perhaps because for some people celibate chastity is the best way to grow. It's their call and their destiny. Those invited to this way of living soon realize that human, sexual, and spiritual growth is possible, often enough with extraordinary results.

As we leave this chapter and move toward our Epilogue, try to keep these key points in mind. First of all, a life of celibate chastity must be rooted deeply in the spiritual life and have significance. Second, many myths and misunderstandings exist about people who live out their sexuality in this manner. Third, celibate chastity entails pursuing and developing ways of loving that are non-genital; is connected vitally to one's call in life and one's call to ministry; entails a way of living wherein one chooses not to be coupled. Fourth, it's experienced at times as the law, a discipline, a functional value, and a gift or gospel value. Finally, discipline, solitude, a sense of humor, and relationships of intimacy are some of its essential ingredients.

Most of all, though, remember this important point: just

as we grow into poverty and obedience, so also do we grow into celibate chastity. Those who come to the end of that journey will realize something that God has known about us for a long time: at the heart of genuine celibate chaste living is union with God and others. In this way those who live out their sexuality in this manner give witness to the world beyond.

REFLECTION QUESTIONS

A final set of questions to help you integrate the material in this chapter. If it's helpful, jot a few notes to yourself in response to each. As always, discussion with others can enrich your reflection.

1. What's at the heart of your celibate chaste living? Spend some time exploring what motivates you to live out your sexuality in this manner. What role, if any, does spirituality really have in your life of celibate chastity?
2. A number of people insist that the spiritual life must be at the heart of genuine celibate chaste living. What does that mean concretely for you in your life of celibate chastity? Please explain.
3. How do Sipe's stages measure up to your own experience? Although he developed them using a small sample of priests, do you see any similar patterns in your own life? If so, in what ways?

REFERENCES

Breckel, Suzanne. *Sexuality, the Celibate's Response.* (Unpublished lecture, National Assembly of Religious Brothers meeting, Providence, RI: 1977).

Coriden, James A. and Thomas J. Green and Donald E. Heintschel. *The Code of Canon Law*. (Mahwah, NJ: Paulist Press, 1985)

Goergen, Donald. *The Sexual Celibate*. (New York, NY: Seabury, 1974).

Levinson, Daniel J. *Seasons of a Man's Life*. (New York, NY: Alfred Knopf, 1978).

Sammon, Sean D. *Growing Pains in Ministry*. (Mystic, CT: Twenty-Third Publications, 1983).

Sipe, A.W. Richard. *The Secret World: Sexuality and the Search for Celibacy*. (New York, NY: Brunner/Mazel, 1990).

EPILOGUE

This book's purpose is very simple: to help men and women called to a life of celibate chastity understand better this way of being a sexual person. First and foremost, it's a tool for education. Until recently, knowledge about human sexuality and celibate chastity was sorely lacking in the lives of some priests, men and women religious, and those single and single again. Sad to say, a shortage of accurate and adequate information about both topics continues to mark the lives of a number of others.

Many topics related to human sexuality and celibate chastity are not discussed in this book. For example, a thorough treatment of psychosexual growth during childhood and the adolescent years is missing. So also are discussions about persons with AIDS in religious life, all the canonical implications of a vow of chastity or promise of celibacy, and a number of other issues. Resources exist that treat these topics. In addition to the references listed at the end of each chapter, I have included at the end of this book a short bibliography that will help interested readers.

I belong to the generation that grew to adulthood in the years following Vatican Council II. We came to maturity during the so-called Sexual Revolution; little in our formation for celibate chastity prepared us for the turmoil of that period in recent history.

In the past, discussions about sexuality and celibate chastity were often marked by embarrassment, awkward silence, and warnings against "particular friendships." That situation needs to change and, thankfully, has in a number of formation centers. More work remains to be done, though, so that a new generation can grow in its appreciation of the gifts of human sexuality and celibate chaste living. Older generations also need some help in this task.

What constitutes adequate education about human sexuality and celibate chastity? First of all, discussion about friendship and relationships of intimacy. If neither were possible in a life of celibate chastity, who would choose this way of living out their human sexuality?

Next, sufficient and correct information about genital sexuality and sexual orientation; emotional, spiritual, and sexual growth over the course of life; and those elements needed for healthy psychosexual growth. Seminary and novitiate formation programs should provide opportunities for men and women to discuss these areas freely and with no fear of reprisal. So also, ongoing education should work toward helping priests, sisters, brothers, and those who are single and single again to talk openly and with ease about the topics listed above.

Finally, a growing appreciation of our relationship with God. That bond is at the heart of mature celibate chaste living. What needs to mark it? Passion, a hunger for God, courage, a spirit of adventure. Passion enough to surrender to God's seductive call; a hunger satisfied only by God's consoling grace; the courage to accept God's way of loving us even when it doesn't mirror our own; a vision of life as an adventure that eventually brings us home.

Passion, then, a hunger for God, courage, a spirit of adventure — all these things are necessary for a life of celibate chastity. Loving friends too must companion us on our journey. God wouldn't have it any other way. Celibate chastity is one wonderful way to live out our sexuality; the lives of hundreds of thousands of priests, sisters, brothers, and single and single again men and women testify to that fact.

APPENDIX

A PASTORAL RESPONSE TO CHILD SEXUAL ABUSE

Why would anyone sexually molest a child? This troubling question lies at the heart of many present-day discussions about sexual abuse. Contemporary scientific knowledge provides neither a simple nor complete answer. The question, however, calls urgently for response. Television documentaries and expanded press coverage about the topic as well as evidence of a 200 percent increase in reported abuse between 1976 and 1987 have caused the public to wonder whether an epidemic of abuse is sweeping the nation.

THE EXPERIENCE OF ABUSE

There is little question that the experience of abuse can be traumatic. Maggie Hoyal, writing in *I Never Told Anyone: Writings by Women Survivors of Child Sexual Abuse*, provides this harrowing account of her abuse: "He pulled his hand out of my pants and spit on his fingers and rubbed them together. He didn't even seem aware of me. The sound of his spitting made me sick. Then he put his hand back down my pants and started to say something in that voice he used.

"The front screen door slammed and his hand ripped out of my pants like it was burned. Then he turned to me and whispered harshly, 'Don't you say anything to your mother ever. If you do, you'll be sorrier than you've ever been in your life.'"

In another example, Mike Lew, psychotherapist and author of *Victims No More: Men Recovering from Incest and Other Sexual Child Abuse*, documents the story of Robert, a twenty-eight-year-old survivor whose adult relationships continue to carry the scars of the incest he suffered as a child. "My father periodically sent me into the bathroom where my mother would be screaming and wailing; he expected me to calm her down and 'take care of her.' It got to the point where she so much counted on me to assuage her painful feelings that she began to have her outbursts in my bedroom. She would get into my bed and wait for me to come into my room and make her feel better. I still remember the smell and feel of her in my bed, and it repulses me.

"She more and more appreciated my attention to the point that she wanted all of it. She didn't want me to date. She told me to watch out for girls because they only had sex on their minds. My girlfriend/romance relationships have been difficult from the beginning. The moment I first start feeling attracted to a female companion, I start to get nauseous. I have vomited my way through every relationship I have ever had that was at all interesting to me."

EXTENT OF THE PROBLEM

The results of recently enacted child abuse reporting laws indicate widespread exploitation of children and adolescents. The problem appears more common than physical abuse. For example, the results of a questionnaire distributed during the late 1970's to a group of college students revealed that prior to their eighteenth birthday nearly one in five of the women and one in eleven of the men had had a sexual experience with an adult.

The increasing number of widely publicized arrests for this behavior has also sensitized the general population. Especially shocking has been the arrest of teachers, child-care workers, and priests and men religious. In these abuse situations, public outrage springs, in part, from the violation of trust.

FIVE QUESTIONS

Church leaders have special pastoral responsibilities when dealing with sexual abuse, particularly if it involves a colleague. Their obligations extend not only to victims, their families, and the perpetrators of abuse, but to all men and women ministering in the Church community who need to continue to do so free of suspicion.

To act responsibly, everyone in Church work needs to learn the facts about child sexual abuse. Comprehensive education, a necessary first step, provides important tools for intervention, treatment, and prevention.

As part of this effort, let's pose and answer five questions:

1. What is child sexual abuse?
2. Who are the victims of this behavior?
3. Who are the perpetrators?
4. What constitutes an adequate assessment of an abuser?
5. What is the outcome of treatment for the perpetrator?

What is child sexual abuse?

Most minors are incapable of freely consenting to sex with an adult. Consequently, sexual involvement between adults and children is widely condemned. Abuse occurs when dependent, developmentally immature children and adolescents become involved in sexual activity which they do not understand fully and to which they cannot give informed consent. This behavior often violates the social taboos of family roles.

Pedophilia, a term meaning literally "love of a child," features prominently in many discussions about sexual abuse. However, L.M. Lothstein, Director of Psychology at the Institute of Living in Hartford, Connecticut stresses the need to distinguish between the terms *pedophilia* and *ephebophilia*. The first refers to an adult who has recurrent, intense sexual urges and sexually arousing fantasies involving a prepubescent child or children. The child's age is arbitrarily set at thirteen years or younger; the adult must be at least five years older than the child. To use the term pedophilia, then, a prepubertal child must be the fantasy object or a participant in the behavior.

Ephebophilia is a term used to refer to an adult who has recurrent, intense sexual urges and sexually arousing fantasies but whose object is a pubescent child or adolescent. The child's age is arbitrarily set at age fourteen through seventeen years; the adult is at least five years older than the child.

Types of abuse

Child sexual abuse falls into several categories: incest, exhibitionism, molestation, rape, sexual sadism, and child pornography and prostitution. Each behavior can be considered pedophilia when a prepubertal child is involved. For example, molestation, a vague term used interchangeably with "indecent liberties," includes fondling, inappropriate touching or kissing, especially in the breast or genital areas, masturbating a youngster, or urging him or her to fondle or masturbate the adult.

Incest, often included under the heading of pedophilia, consists of any physical sexual activity between family members. The term family is used here in a broad sense. The presence or absence of a blood relationship between incest participants is of far less significance than the kinship roles they occupy. The activity can occur between a child and parent, stepparent, extended family member (for example, grandparent, brother-in-law, aunt) or surrogate parent (for example, foster parent).

Exhibitionism, child pornography, and child prostitution are other types of abuse. Exhibitionism usually involves an adult male's exposure of his genitals to girls, boys, and women. One exhibitionist may walk exposed in shopping malls, school yards, and other open spaces; another drives or parks his car with his pants pulled down. Both experience sexual excitement from the shock or surprise of onlookers.

While conventional wisdom maintains that exhibitionists are not violent, a significant number of child rapists have also practiced exhibitionism.

Child pornography includes the arranging of video photography or film production of sexual acts between minors and other children, adults, or animals, regardless of consent by the child's legal guardian. The distribution of such material in any form, whether profit making or not, is legally prohibited.

Child prostitution involves boys and girls in sex acts for profit, often with frequently changing partners. Approximately 300,000 children in the United States are involved in child pornography and prostitution.

Sexual abuse, then, is a broad term describing sexual activity involving both prepubertal and pubescent children. Victims are unable to give informed consent to these behaviors and do not comprehend fully their consequences. Only when a prepubescent child is involved should pedophilia, a more restricted technical term, be used.

Pattern of abuse

Child abuse expert Suzanne Sgroi points out that sexual encounters between adults and children usually follow a predictable pattern: engagement, sexual interaction, secrecy, disclosure, and suppression. During the engagement phase, perpetrators of abuse often look for opportunities to be alone with the child and engage in sexual activity.

The interaction phase often includes the progression of sexual activities: exposure, fondling, and possibly some form of penetration. Any of these behaviors might be accompanied by ejaculation.

After the victimization, most perpetrators try to impose secrecy. It eliminates accountability and enables repetition of the behavior.

Disclosure interrupts the secrecy phase. External circumstances can accidentally lead to the secret becoming known. For example, the abusive activity may be observed by a third party. Physical injury to the child, pregnancy, symptoms of a sexually transmitted disease, or the child's initiation of sexually precocious behavior can also draw outside attention to the victimization.

Some participants decide to tell outsiders about the abuse. A young child, for example, finding the behavior exciting or stimulating, shares the secret. An adolescent girl's father, wanting his sexual needs met, curtails his daughter's peer and social activities and has her stay within the family circle. Out of frustration she reveals their incestuous relationship.

Following the disclosure her feelings may be mixed: relief, disloyalty for betraying her father, anger, guilt if she enjoyed aspects of the relationship. Disclosure offers the possibility of planned intervention.

TWO REACTIONS

While perpetrators usually respond with alarm to the secret's revelation, family members ask: "How will this situation affect me?" Those who are secure and possess emotional strength move toward the victim with concern and protection; others, already aware of the abuse or perhaps participants in it, react with guilt or out of self-interest. Families need enormous support to maintain a victim-oriented response.

How do siblings react to disclosure? In two ways usually: with concern for the victim, and/or anger at the perpetrator. Some may have suffered abuse themselves. However, when victimization occurs at the hands of someone outside the family, brothers and sisters can resent the disruption in family life, the exposure and publicity resulting from disclosure.

Finally, the extended family can display this combination of reactions to the abuse: protection and concern for the child along with defensiveness and self-protection. Some family members may pressure others to react with denial, and fail to cooperate with child-protection agencies or law enforcement authorities.

A suppression phase often follows disclosure. Whether the abuse happened within or outside the family, members try to suppress publicity, information, and intervention. Some deny the significance of the disturbance suffered by the victim and discourage further intervention by outsiders.

When the abuse occurs within the family, suppression can be intense. The perpetrator tries to undermine the child's credibility and the allegation of sexual victimization. The victim might be described as a pathological liar or mentally disturbed. Threats of separation and verbal and physical abuse may be used to pressure the child to recant or stop cooperating with the intervention process. Other family members can "gang up" on the youngster who is made to feel guilty for disclosing the secret. Feeling isolated and alone, some victims withdraw the complaint or stop cooperating with those trying to assist.

Ellen Bass and Laura Davis, writing in *Courage to Heal*, tell the story of Carey to illustrate the wrath some victims suffer following disclosure. "When I was eleven, I went horseback riding with my best girlfriend. I told my girlfriend what I was doing with my stepfather. She told her mother, who called my mother. When I got home, my mother came tearing out of the house, crazy angry. She grabbed me and pulled me off my horse. Kicking me and hitting me, she dragged me into the house, up the steps, across the porch, into my bedroom. She threw me on the bed, screaming at me about telling stories.

"I was sobbing and saying, 'They're not stories, they're true, and you know they're true.' And she started to choke me. My stepfather was standing right behind her, watching, with no expression on his face.

"I couldn't breathe. I believe she would have killed me. It was the third time she tried. Finally he pulled her off, saying, 'You know nobody's going to believe her. Nobody believes anything she says.'"

VICTIMS

Victims of child sexual abuse come from all races, creeds, and socioeconomic levels. A victim might be white, red, yellow, or black, Catholic or Protestant, rich or poor. The child may be either a boy or girl, although for every boy, two or three girls are reportedly victimized.

Although infants and young children suffer abuse, Finkelhor points out that exploitation often begins at age eight or nine, and lasts about five years. Interestingly, boys are more commonly victimized by someone outside their family. Some children are threatened with punishment if they fail to cooperate; others are manipulated and told the activity is a game or something "special" or fun.

Child abuse specialist Adele Mayer notes that many child victims exhibit a pseudo-maturity that masks their need for normal parental affection. They are also marked by feelings of guilt and responsibility; some believe that they could have done something to prevent the incest or stop it once it started. Eventually, victims lose trust in authority figures.

Abuse suffered in childhood has serious consequences for adult living. Victims experience a variety of problems as they seek mature adult relationships of intimacy. Their need for nurturance is often thwarted and many have difficulties with trust and responsibility. The repressed rage of a number of victims also results in a variety of self-destructive behaviors including suicide threats and attempts, self-mutilation, and chemical and alcohol abuse.

Adult survivors are often left with an impaired sense of reality. Failing to understand what goes on in their world, they grow to distrust themselves and others. Most live by this motto: "If I imagine that it's not happening, maybe it will go away." Eventually, a number pretend that some things are just not happening.

Some people ask, "How can I tell if I was a victim of child sexual abuse?" Abuse therapists Ellen Bass and Laura Davis provide this checklist. As a child or teenager, were you touched in sexual areas; shown sexual movies or forced to listen to sexual talk; made to pose for seductive or sexual photographs; subjected to unnecessary medical treatments; forced to perform oral sex on an adult or sibling; raped or otherwise penetrated; fondled, kissed, or held in a way that made you feel uncomfortable; forced to take part in ritualized abuse in which you were physically or sexually tortured; made to watch sexual acts or look at sexual parts; bathed in a way that felt intrusive to you; objectified and ridiculed about your body; encouraged or goaded into sex you didn't really want; told all you were good for was sex; involved in child prostitution or pornography?

Bass and Davis suggest that adult survivors often go to great lengths to deny what happened to them. One woman convinced herself it was all a dream; another dismissed her memory. Still another spoke these words about her struggle with denial: "I did not want to believe what had happened. Even as part of me recognized the truth, another part fought to deny what I had seen. There were times when I would rather have viewed myself as crazy than acknowledge what had happened to me."

For abuse survivors, however, denial is often a necessary stage in the process of dealing with traumatic pain. It provides respite when they cannot bear to align themselves with the small, wounded child inside. Denial allows survivors to function day to day; it also permits them to set their own pace of recovery.

Bass and Davis also list these additional destructive ways in which survivors cope: minimizing (pretending that what happened really wasn't that bad); rationalizing (explaining away the abuse — "Oh, he couldn't help it; he was drunk"); denying that anything happened; leaving the body (numbing the body so that the child does not feel what is being done to him or her); splitting (that feeling of being divided into more than one person); spacing-out (the capacity to not be present); chaos (maintaining control by creating disorder); super-alertness; humor; busyness; forgetting (many children forget the abuse even as it is happening to them).

An anonymous author, writing in *Slayer of the Soul: Child Sexual Abuse and the Catholic Church*, provides this description of her attempts to "forget" the abuse she suffered. "I don't remember much. Actually, I don't want to remember. It is not a conscious decision. Sometimes, I say to myself, 'Listen, you need to look at this; you will feel a lot better if you do.' But my insides resound with almost a scream, 'No!' My therapist says that it is normal for an adult who was abused as a child not to remember — a type of amnesia. Well, I have definitely got amnesia."

What about recovery? Though abuse victims face many obstacles in this process, they should never forget these two points: help is available and healing is possible. Mayer points out that semi-structured groups focusing on both experiential and didactic work are one of the most effective tools for healing. Survivors identify readily with one another; their shared empathy is immediate, powerful, and very therapeutic. No matter how people recall their history of abuse, it's important to talk with others about it. No one can heal alone.

The "Unsent Letter to the Offender" is another powerful help to recovery. Its instructions are clear: the survivor writes a letter to their abuser. In it they express their feelings about the person, the abuse that was perpetrated, and the effects that it has had on them and their life. The writer then reads the letter aloud to the other members of their group, often repeatedly, until their verbal expression equals the intensity of the content.

Whatever means are used for healing, Mayer suggests that all must have these six outcomes as their goal: validate individual worth; share with others the commonality of the abuse experience and its aftermath; decrease guilt, self-blame, and responsibility for the abuse on the part of the victim; impart educational information; teach assertive behavior; release blocked emotions, thus assisting in their identification.

Reporting abuse

In the past, most exploitation went unreported. During the late 1970's, however, the reporting of abuse cases grew sharply, giving a more realistic picture of the extent and nature of the problem. The American Humane Association, a national organization collecting child abuse data, documented an increase in reported cases from 1,975 in 1976 to 22,918 in 1983. This rapid increase can be explained in part by this fact: not until 1978 did all U.S. states participate in data gathering.

Other sources reflect previously unimagined widespread abuse. In a meticulous 1978 survey conducted in San Francisco, 38 percent of the women questioned reported unwanted sexual touching, and attempted or completed forcible rape prior to age eighteen.

Parents' characteristics

Child abuse researcher David Finkelhor illustrates the small fraction of abuses actually reported with this projection: if no more than 10 percent of all girls and 2 percent of all boys were abused sexually, roughly 210,000 new cases should be occurring each year. This figure is considerably greater than the actual number of reported cases.

While lack of peer friendships can be a predicator of sexual abuse, certain characteristics of a child's parents are strongly associated with victimization.

1. Having a stepfather more than doubles a girl's vulnerability to abuse.
2. A courting mother who brings sexually exploitative men into the home also increases her daughter's risk of victimization.
3. Fathers who show their daughters little physical affection and believe strongly in children's obedience and the subordination of women increase the risk of abuse. The child fails to discriminate between genuine affection and thinly disguised sexual interest,

subordinating herself unquestionably to an abuser's wish.

4. Girls living without their natural mother often lack adequate supervision. Mothers working outside the home, however, do not generally place their daughters at greater risk.
5. Poor mother-daughter communication and mothers who are punitive about sexual matters increase a daughter's risk. Girls bombarded with sexual prohibitions and punishments may have a hard time developing informed and realistic standards about what constitutes abuse.
6. Women who feel powerless and victimized communicate these attitudes to their daughters.
7. Significant discrepancies between the mother's educational background and that of her husband can increase a daughter's victimization risk. A well-educated father and a mother who is not constitutes the most dangerous parental combination. A wife with substantially less education can feel subordinate to her husband and dependent upon him. Her daughter may learn this lesson: she too is powerless and must obey.

While not a checklist, a significant number of these factors in a girl's life puts adults on alert about the possibility of abuse.

Are boys also at risk for abuse? Definitely. Finkelhor estimates that between 46,000 and 92,000 boys under the age of thirteen are victimized each year. However, few cases reach public attention. Boys grow up with an ethic of self-reliance to fight their own battles. When hurt they seek help less readily.

Other reasons explain the underreporting of abused boys.

1. Youthful male sexuality is portrayed in positive, adventuresome terms and boys' sexual experiences

with adults are often judged to be less victimizing than they are in fact.

2. Adolescent males abused by men, especially those with questions about their masculinity, fear being labeled homosexual if others discover their victimization.
3. Boys have more to lose from reporting abuse than girls. Their freedom and independence, generally greater than that of girls, may be curtailed by parents and guardians. Consequently, older boys in particular tend to report less.

Our culture provides little room for the notion of men as victims; after all, few people realized that *The Summer of '42* was a film about child abuse — that's right, child abuse. An adolescent boy became involved with an older woman. Mike Lew points out that "real men" are supposed to possess the ability to protect themselves, solve any problem, and recover from any setback. When men experience victimization, our culture expects them to "deal with it like a man."

Who victimizes children?

About 85 percent of all abusers are male, from every profession and trade, skilled and unskilled. Many are described as "me first" individuals who find sexual relationships with children safer — less threatening, demanding, and problematic.

Sexual encounters between adults and minors cover a wide spectrum. Finkelhor points out that they include the man who spends his whole life fixated on eight-year-old boys, and another who convinces his girlfriend to bring a child into their bed to "experience something new." Children are the sole erotic interest of some adults; others become involved only under extraordinary situational circumstances.

Child sex offenders can be divided into two basic types: fixated and regressed. At the outset of sexual maturation, fixated abusers develop an exclusive attraction to children. Although they may engage in sexual activity with persons their own age, and even marry, these sexual relationships are usually initiated by the other party, result from social pressure, or provide access to children.

Are regressed offenders predisposed initially toward sexual involvement with children? No. However, when adulthood's conflictual relationships, responsibilities, and misfortunes overwhelm them, the primary focus of their sexual interest moves from persons their own age to minors. Psychologically the fixated offender becomes like a child; for the regressed offender, the child is a pseudo-adult.

Four factors

Few child abuse theories address the behavior's full complexity. Some adults who are sexually aroused by children never act on these impulses. They have alternative sources of gratification or may be inhibited by ordinary social controls.

Finkelhor identifies four factors, framed as questions, that, to one extent or another, contribute to the making of a child abuser.

1. *Emotional congruence.* Why does a person find relating sexually to a child emotionally gratifying and congruent?
2. *Sexual arousal to children.* Why is a person capable of being sexually aroused by a child?
3. *Blockage.* Why is a person blocked in efforts to get his

or her emotional and sexual needs met in adult relationships?

4. *Disinhibition.* Why is a person not deterred by conventional social inhibitions from having a sexual relationship with a child?

Does each factor play an equal role in the life of every abuser? Probably not. These questions, however, provide a starting point in searching out an explanation for the causes of abuse.

1. *Why does a person find relating sexually to a child emotionally gratifying and congruent?*

For some people a "fit" exists between their emotional needs and the child's characteristics. Arrested psychological development leaves them feeling like children. Having childish emotional needs, they wish to relate to other children.

In addition to their immaturity, a number of victimizers have low self-esteem and feel inadequate in their social relationships with adults. Their interactions with minors provide them with feelings of power, omnipotence, and control.

For others, child-molesting fantasies help overcome the shame, humiliation, or powerlessness they experienced as a small child at the hands of an adult. A large number of abusers were victimized as children. In "identifying with the aggressor" they achieve symbolic mastery over childhood-induced psychological trauma.

Answering the question from a different perspective, feminist explanations point to themes in male socialization that make children "appropriate" sexual partners. Men are taught to be dominant, powerful, and the initiator in sexual relationships. As a consequence, many are socialized to relate to sexual partners who are younger, smaller, and weaker than themselves.

2. *Why is a person capable of being sexually aroused by a child?*

Many adults have an emotional need to relate to children. They may want to be with children, love or control children, or have the youngsters dependent upon them. These men and women meet their need in nonsexual ways by becoming parents, teachers, child care workers, pediatricians, and such. Child sexual victimization needs an explanation independent of, or in addition to, having a strong emotional need to relate to minors.

Abusers show unusual levels of arousal to children. Researchers look to two areas to explain this finding: biological factors and social learning theory.

Biological factors, such as chromosomal make-up or hormone level, appear to be a source of instability that may predispose a person to develop a deviant pattern of sexual arousal. Physiological abnormalities have been found among some victimizers. Drs. Fred Berlin and John Money of Johns Hopkins University report success in treating them with anti-androgenic drugs such as Depo-provera. This theory about the origin of abuse, however, needs further development to explain why a child is selected as the object of sexual arousal.

Social learning theory suggests that a fixation with children originates with an early arousal experience incorporated into a repeated fantasy that, in subsequent masturbatory experiences, becomes increasingly more arousing. The reinforcement associated with masturbation links pleasure with the victimization fantasy.

Other social learning theorists claim the abuse experienced may not be so important in childhood victimization as is being provided with a model who finds children sexually stimulating. Child pornography and advertising which sexualizes minors also play a possible role in abuse. The pleasure experienced by adults masturbating to this material is reinforcing; eventually they may come to find children arousing.

3. *Why is a person blocked in efforts to get his or her emotional and sexual needs met in adult relationships?*

Two types of blocks exist: developmental and situational. The first prevents a person from moving into an adult stage of psychosexual development. For example, some abusers are timid, inadequate, and awkward individuals who lack the social skills necessary for adult relationships while others, associating adult sexuality with pain and rejection, choose children as a safer substitute source of gratification.

Repressive sexual norms may also operate causing the abuser guilt and conflict about engaging in adult sexual relationships. Some researchers describe child victimizers as among the most repressed of all offenders.

With situational blocks a person with apparent adult sexual interests is cut off from normal sexual outlets due to the loss of a relationship or some other transitory crisis. In incest families, for example, a man's relationship with his wife has often deteriorated.

4. *Why is a person not deterred by conventional social inhibitions from having a sexual relationship with a child?*

Personality and situational factors are often cited to answer this question. For example, a small number of offenders have poor impulse control. Consequently, they easily overcome inhibitions against acting on abuse impulses. Alcohol and alcoholism and other chemical dependencies are significant factors in abuse. While not causing victimization, they do make its commission easier.

Situational factors can reduce inhibitions about abuse. Loss of employment, the death of a loved one, or a period of great personal stress are factors in a number of victimizations. Being a stepdaughter may also reduce the usual inhibitions about sexual activity between a girl and her father.

Feminist theories about abuse cite certain social and cultural elements that weaken inhibitions by encouraging or condoning sexual behavior directed toward children. Social approval for the excesses of patriarchal and parental authority is a factor here. Blaming victims for abuse, the criminal justice system's past reluctance to prosecute and punish offenders, and the present-day failure of some institutions to respond quickly and knowledgeably to reports of victimization are seen by others as "green lights" for abuse.

Finally, as mentioned in Chapter III, psychologist Patrick Carnes coined the phrase "sexual addiction" to explain some sexually compulsive behavior. Alcoholism has this common definition: a person has a pathological relationship to a mood-altering chemical. Sex addicts substitute a pathological relationship to a mood-altering experience for healthier relationships with others.

The addiction begins with delusional thought processes rooted in the addict's belief system. Four core beliefs distort reality: "I am basically a bad, unworthy person"; "No one would love me as I am"; "My needs are never going to be met if I have to depend on others"; and "Sex is my most important need." Sexual addiction can overcome the conventional social inhibitions about having sex with a child.

Finkelhor's four-factor model, cited earlier, helps to explain why many people with important prerequisite components for engaging in abuse never do. While they may fulfill the requirement of one or two factors, they differ from perpetrators who meet the requirement for all four factors.

What constitutes adequate evaluation of an abuser?

Any evaluation of a child abuser needs to be comprehensive and to involve specialists from a number of different disciplines. An adequate assessment includes these elements: a physical examination with additional lab work to discover disorders that may be contributing to the behavior (kidney and liver function tests, routine chromosomal analysis); detailed neurological examination, and neuro-psychological testing to rule out seizure activity or other neurological pathology; comprehensive psychological testing; a complete sexual history; comprehensive addiction evaluation, including assessment for sexual addiction; a thorough spiritual history to assess possible resources for treatment; clinical interviewing conducted by specialists familiar with the area of child sexual abuse.

The evaluation's results and recommendations need to be explained thoroughly to the perpetrator and, with his or her permission, others involved in the treatment.

WHAT TREATMENT EXISTS FOR PERPETRATORS OF ABUSE? WHAT IS ITS OUTCOME?

What causes child sexual abuse? We do not know fully. Treatment can be difficult. Offenders often deny their predisposition and activity and minimize its effects.

Helping perpetrators of abuse does not condone their behavior. It needs to stop. However, a more informed understanding about the problem and effective interventions are sorely needed.

Who needs education? Several groups: Church ministers; families; medical, psychiatric, and social service personnel; law enforcement authorities; and members of the criminal justice system. Fred Berlin points out that until recently, each generation also produced contagious carriers of smallpox. Many died. Prevention came about not by punishing, imprisoning, or exiling carriers. Research found the cause of smallpox, controlled it with vaccination and, by 1979, wiped it out completely.

While child sexual abuse may never be eliminated completely, continued investigation into its causes and consequences and helpful interventions can go a long way toward reducing the frequency and extent of exploitation.

Treatment for sexual abuse has to be many-sided. Individual talking therapy is not sufficient. A comprehensive program is called for and must include these elements: individual and group therapy; sex education; behavioral and cognitive therapies; re-socialization to enhance interpersonal skills; tension reduction training for the management of anxiety and anger; anti-anxiety, anti-depressant, and/or anti-androgen (Depo-provera, Cyproterone acetate) medications; victim personalization groups; and self-help groups such as Sex and Love Addicts Anonymous (S.L.A.A.), Sexaholics Anonymous (S.A.), or Sex Addicts Anonymous (S.A.A.). An extended period of aftercare must also follow any residential treatment.

A closer look at three treatment components illustrates part of the range of available interventions: anti-androgen medications, victim personalization, and self-help groups. To begin with, anti-androgen drugs suppress the sexual appetite in general. They do not leave conventional sexual desires intact while decreasing others that are deviant. Depo-provera's short-term side effects can include weight gain, mild lethargy, nightmares, hot flashes, cold sweats, hypertension, shortness of breath, shrunken testicle size, elevated blood sugar, and decreased sperm count with remaining sperm possibly being atypical.

Apparently these effects can be reversed by stopping the medication. The results of animal studies have also reported malignant breast tumors. Long-term effects of the medication need further study.

Next, the majority of offenders deny the harm they do or the risk they pose for their victims. They maintain the illusion that the child welcomed, appreciated, and may even have benefitted from the sexual encounter.

Victim personalization groups focus on the impact on the

victim of various types of sexual offenses. Attention is given to the abuse's immediate and long-term aftereffects. Group members come to realize more fully why victims behave as they do and how their lives are affected by the victimization.

Finally, self-help groups modeled after Alcoholics Anonymous are an available treatment resource. Their approach is based on A.A.'s "Twelve Steps." While no statistics presently exist about the long-term effectiveness of participation in these groups, members' personal testimony leaves little doubt about their importance for people formerly without hope.

Overcoming the perpetrator's attempts to deny and minimize the abuse that has occurred is a challenge for therapists. The comments of a convicted priest child abuser, writing anonymously in *Slayer of the Soul: Child Sexual Abuse and the Catholic Church*, illustrate this point: "I knew that in my true character I was not the person who would have acted this way. My true character would not have done that. So the lie of my life became apparent. I had a lot of trouble accepting that lie, that I was a child abuser."

Can anyone guarantee that following treatment an offender will never again abuse a child? No. The past decade, though, has witnessed some helpful advances in the treatment of this disorder.

When is the best time for an abuser to get help? Today. Even for those who have never acted on their impulses, assistance is available. Optimally, they can be helped before any child is victimized.

PASTORAL RECOMMENDATIONS

Attorney F. Ray Mouton, speaking at a seminar entitled "Suffer the Children: Sexual Misconduct of Ministers in the Catholic Community," made this comment: "We must remember at all times that children are entrusted to us, all of us, by

God, and when a perpetrator sexually molests a child, be that person a layperson, a cleric or religious, the very first thing that is taken from that child is that which is God's greatest gift, innocence."

Even though new reporting laws have increased sensitivity to the victimization of minors, child sexual abuse continues to be vastly underreported. Whether the behavior occurs within or outside the home, at the hands of parents, relatives, family friends, or strangers, Church ministers need to assist abuse victims and their families. Serving as administrators, pastors, teachers, health care workers, and counselors, they are ideally situated to observe possible abuse situations and arrange for intervention and treatment.

Church ministers are also obliged to protect possible future victims. Swift and responsible action in any current abuse situation can prevent later tragedy for others.

Some necessary steps

Child sexual victimization unreported and untreated early in life needs later attention. Church people need to help abuse victims address this painful experience during the adult years and find resources for healing.

A pastoral response starts with education about the problem and what can be done about it. These efforts should extend not only to ministers but to families, students, and parishioners as well. Dioceses and religious communities also need to develop plans for evaluation and intervention to handle reports of victimization. In undertaking this effort, professional clinical *and* legal advice should be sought.

When the abuser is a priest or religious prompt and informed action is just as necessary. Religious leaders have these responsibilities to perpetrators of abuse: investigate any suspicion of abuse; adhere to the letter and spirit of state reporting laws; make available to the abuser adequate evaluation, treatment, and legal assistance.

Those in leadership have additional responsibilities to victims of abuse and the perpetrator's fellow ministers. First of all, victims of abuse and their families merit a pastoral response from the Church. Any assistance needed with treatment should, of course, be provided; victims and their families also need to be assured, by word and action, that the perpetrator will not victimize again.

Second, fellow ministers need protection from guilt by association. Stated simply, they must be provided the opportunity to continue their ministry free of suspicion.

CONCLUSION

The person who becomes sexually involved with children is scorned, stigmatized, and condemned. Few people apparently wish to discover the behavior's cause, let alone show compassion or forgiveness and provide help. Today, the Church community can provide leadership by recalling that in this situation, as in so many others, Jesus' message mitigates revenge in favor of decisive action, compassion, forgiveness, and reformation.

REFERENCES

Bass, Ellen and Laura Davis. *The Courage to Heal: A Guide for Women Survivors of Child Sexual Abuse*. (New York, NY: Harper and Row, 1988).

Bass, Ellen and Louise Thornton. *I Never Told Anyone: Writings by Women Survivors of Child Sexual Abuse*. (New York, NY: Harper and Row, 1983).

Carnes, Patrick. *Out of the Shadows: Understanding Sexual Addiction*. (Minneapolis, MN: CompCare Publishers, 1983).

Finkelhor, David. *Child Sexual Abuse: New Theory and Research*. (New York, NY: FreePress, 1984).

Lew, Mike. *Victims No Longer: Men Recovering from Incest and Other Sexual Child Abuse*. (New York: NY: Harper Collins, 1990).

Mayer, Adele. *Sexual Abuse: Causes, Consequences and Treatment of Incestuous and Pedophilic Acts*. (Holmes Beach, FL: Learning Publications, 1985).

Rossetti, Stephen J. (ed.). *Slayer of the Soul: Child Sexual Abuse and the Catholic Church*. (Mystic, CT: Twenty-Third Publications, 1990).

BIBLIOGRAPHY

CAHILL, LISA SOWLE. *Women and Sexuality*. (Mahwah, NJ: Paulist, 1992).

CLARK, KEITH. *Being Sexual... and Celibate*. (Notre Dame, IN: Ave Maria Press, 1986).

CLARK, KEITH. *An Experience of Celibacy*. (Notre Dame, IN: Ave Maria Press, 1982).

COLEMAN, GERALD D., S.S. *Human Sexuality: An All-Embracing Gift*. (Staten Island, NY: Alba House, 1992).

CONFERENCE OF MAJOR SUPERIORS OF MEN. *Shadow on the Family: AIDS in Religious Life*. (Silver Spring, MD: Conference of Major Superiors of Men, 1987).

DE CASTILLEJO, IRENE CLAREMONT. *Knowing Woman*. (New York, NY: Harper and Row, 1973).

FERDER, FRAN AND JOHN HEAGLE. *Your Sexual Self: Pathways to Authentic Intimacy*. (Notre Dame, IN: Ave Maria Press, 1992).

GREELEY, ANDREW. *Sexual Intimacy*. (Chicago, IL: Thomas More, 1973).

GROESCHEL, BENEDICT. *The Courage to Be Chaste*. (Ramsey, NJ: Paulist, 1985).

HELLDORFER, MARTIN. (ED.) *Sexuality and Brotherhood*. (Lockport, IL: Christian Brothers' Conference, 1977).

HUDDLESON, MARY ANNE. (ed.) *Celibate Loving*. (Ramsey, NJ: Paulist, 1984).

MILLER, JEAN BAKER. *Towards a New Psychology of Women*. (Boston, MA: Beacon Press, 1976).

NELSON, JAMES. *Intimate Connections: Male Sexuality and Masculine Spirituality*. (Philadelphia, PA: Westminster, 1988).

RUBIN, LILLIAN. *Intimate Strangers: Men and Women Together*. (New York, NY: Harper and Row, 1983).

SAMMON, SEAN D. *Sexuality, Celibate Chastity, and the Life Cycle*. (Canfield, OH: Alba House Cassettes).

SCHNEIDERS, SANDRA. *New Wineskins: Re-imagining Religious Life Today*. (Ramsey, NJ: Paulist, 1986).

TYRRELL, THOMAS J. *Urgent Longings*. (Whitinsville, MA: Affirmation Books, 1980).